CHURCHILL'S GERMAN ARMY

Volume 54, Sage Library of Social Research

SAGE LIBRARY OF SOCIAL RESEARCH

CHURCHILL'S GERMAN ARMY

Wartime Strategy and Cold War Politics, 1943-1947

ARTHUR L. SMITH, Jr.

Preface by ALEXANDER DeCONDE

Volume 54
SAGE LIBRARY OF
SOCIAL RESEARCH

SAGE PUBLICATIONS   Beverly Hills/London

Copyright © 1977 by Sage Publications, Inc.

For information address:

SAGE PUBLICATIONS, INC.
275 South Beverly Drive
Beverly Hills, California 90212

SAGE PUBLICATIONS LTD
28 Banner Street
London EC1Y 8QE

Printed in the United States of America

Library of Congress Cataloging in Publication Data

Smith, Arthur Lee, 1927-
    Churchill's German army.

    (Sage library of social research ; v. 54)
    Bibliography: p. 147
    Includes index.
    1. World politics—1945-1955. 2. Germany—
Defenses. 3. Churchill, Winston Leonard Spencer,
Sir, 1874-1965. I. Title.
D842.S547   940.53'22   77-12683
ISBN 0-8039-0928-4
ISBN 0-8039-0929-2 pbk.

FIRST PRINTING

CONTENTS

Cover Illustration from Second World War German Poster

To Bill and Scott

PREFACE

In recent years no other subject has attracted more controversy or engaged the attention of diplomatic historians more intently than how the Cold War started and who should bear responsibility for launching it. Conventional interpretations place origin in 1947 and blame on an aggressive Russia. Revisionist historians, particularly of radical persuasion, challenge this view. Although they do not all adhere to one interpretation, revisionists generally push Cold War origins back beyond 1947 and insist that the United States was as intransigent and therefore at least as blameworthy as the Soviet Union for creating the confrontation.

Professor Arthur L. Smith's study questions both the conventional and revisionist hypotheses. He explains that even before the end of the Second World War Prime Minister Winston Churchill, motivated by a pre-war distrust of Communists that had not diminished even while Great Britain was allied to the Soviet Union, feared an aggressive Russia and believed that Western Europe could not be defended without rearmed German soldiers. Smith suggests that in 1945 Churchill acted on this assumption in preparing Britain for the possibility of facing Russia alone. Of course, Churchill felt confident that ultimately the United States would support him. Thus, in Smith's thesis Great Britain initiated the Cold War against the Soviet Union and did so before the Second World War had ended. Churchill, he indicates, was willing to use former enemy soldiers to carry out his anti-Soviet policy. Since Britain lacked the power to maintain such a policy alone, and in 1947-48 her policy merged with American policy, scholars have focused on Soviet-American animosity and have either ignored or overlooked the British role in the origins of the Cold War.

Smith compensates for this neglect by concentrating on the British position and thereby adds another dimension to Cold War historiography. He has written the kind of speculative analysis, based on wide reading and thorough knowledge of sources, that modern historians admire. His book should also appeal to any reader interested in the subject, for he advances a provocative thesis and in gracious prose tells a stimulating story.

Santa Barbara, California   *Alexander DeConde*

ACKNOWLEDGMENTS

In ways both large and small a variety of people helped me during my research and writing, and it is with great pleasure that I express my gratitude to the following archivists, historians, librarians, and other experts who provided me with either information, advice and/or opinion: Mr. Leif Wold, Lt. Col. Nils Borchgrevink, Dr. H. Brausch, Dr. A. Hoch, Mr. A. Harrington, Mr. Gary Ryan, Dr. Robert Wolfe, Rev. R. A. Graham S.J., Mr. K. Hiscock, Gen. S. L. A. Marshall, Dr. Juergen Rohwer, Dr. H. Meier-Welcker, Admiral Karl Doenitz, Mr. John Lewis, and Dr. Richard Burns. Also, thanks to my editor at Sage, Mr. Lars Jensen. All errors are my responsibility.

A sabbatical leave and an institutional grant from California State University, Los Angeles provided me with time and support to complete my writing during the fall quarter of 1976, and for this I am most appreciative. A special thanks to my wife for enduring with patience and grace my periods of preoccupation with work when I had promised vacation.

July 1977
Los Angeles   *Arthur L. Smith, Jr.*

Chapter 1

THE WOODFORD SPEECH

On November 23, 1954, a number of people from Winston Churchill's constituency of Woodford gathered to present a gift to his wife. It was a natural enough occasion for the old Prime Minister, now nearing his eightieth birthday, to make a few appropriate remarks. Reflecting current political concerns, Churchill wandered briefly over the past ten years, observing that partnerships changed with time and conditions, and that what would have been the cause for disbelief a decade ago was different now. The Prime Minister said that there were persons who had been alerted to the growing dangers on the international scene well before this time pointing out that he himself had warned the House of Commons in 1950 that Europe could not be defended without a rearmed Germany. The response to his warning, he bitterly recalled, was to brand his statement as irresponsible.[1]

Suddenly warming to his subject, Churchill astounded his audience by declaring that, "Even before the war had ended and while the Germans were surrendering by hundreds of thousands, and our streets were crowded with cheering people, I telegraphed to Lord Montgomery directing him to be careful in collecting the German arms, to stack them so that they could easily be issued again to the German soldiers whom we should have to work with if the Soviet advance continued."[2]

Although the Prime Minister's explosive bit of news was almost instantly excused by some observers as a sort of impulsive mischief characteristic of Churchill at times, this was not entirely true. His friend and physician, Lord Moran, recalled that day in November in some detail. The doctor remembered that Churchill had specifically mentioned to him upcoming speeches—including the one at the girl's school in Woodford—for which he needed something interesting and newsworthy. "It seems that he found everyone at Woodford full of the birthday [on November 30]," Moran wrote. "There was a lot of celebrating and drinking of toasts, his foresight was extolled. Then someone asked him about the Russians. . . . He was resolved to make it known that he wanted to take precautions against some rather ugly possibilities as early as the spring of 1945, at a time when the Americans were still busy making friends with Stalin and had not yet woken up to the danger of Communism."[3] Quite clearly the Prime Minister had opened a Pandora's box!

Understandably, as the costar in this historical drama, Field Marshal Montgomery immediately became the object of newspaper attention. At that precise moment, the elderly war hero was on a visit to America, invited by General Eisenhower to speak at Columbia University. When asked about the amazing piece of information that his old friend had thrown out at Woodford the evening before, Montgomery, true to soldierly form, instantly replied, "I obeyed my orders!" While appearing surprised by it all, he declined further comment except to repeat, "It's true."[4] *The Times* ran a similar account for its English readers quoting the Field Marshal as saying, "I received a telegram, but I'm not saying what happened." He greeted a question on the dumping of German military equipment into the sea with a smile.[5]

Naturally, the world's press had differing reactions to the Woodford speech ranging from puzzlement and dismay to anger, bitterness, and in certain quarters, praise and admiration. "Could he have expected memories and emotions to fade overnight?" asked *The Times.*[6] The paper probably reflected the thinking of many Englishmen by wondering aloud just why Churchill had chosen to say what he did. It was true that the Russians had become a menace, but surely it defied all reason to suggest that Englishmen were ready to join the Germans in 1945.[7]

Running briefly through the foreign press reactions, *The Times* reported the French as relatively unconcerned, while the Russians were incensed and blamed Churchill for encouraging the German attack in 1941. In the United States, Bernard Baruch was quoted in support of his old friend, "I have never known him to make an ignoble proposal."[8] Curiously, the German press comments were rather mild with statements like, "Churchill has said too much this time!"[9] or "Churchill airs war secret."[10] One German paper suggested that Churchill's telegram had been responsible for the widespread belief in the German army at the end of the war that it would be joined by the West to fight Russia.[11]

Almost immediately, the Prime Minister was challenged by a Parliament member to publish the message or messages—for Churchill was also quoted as having sent a telegram to General Eisenhower similar to that dispatched to Montgomery.[12] On Thursday, November 25, the Prime Minister's printed answer was that the Eisenhower message was already in print, for it had appeared in Volume six of his work, *The Second World War*, and he provided the appropriate citations.[13] The message to Eisenhower, sent on May 9, 1945, made no reference to either using or rearming German troops.

Churchill had delivered his few remarks at Woodford on a Tuesday evening and to all intents and purposes, while the world had given momentary attention, the entire episode seemed destined for oblivion by the end of the week. Parliament appeared in a forgiving mood, and opposition leader Clement Attlee gave no indication of pressing the issue, although one M.P., Barbara Castle, announced her cancellation to Churchill's birthday party.[14]

No doubt there was broad confusion about what Churchill had said and what he actually meant. He had made reference to messages or telegrams and had already explained that the material was in the public domain and was published in his own work. Many readers accepted the Prime Minister's account at face value and in view of the coming birthday celebration and the enormous reputation of the man himself, there did not seem to be any interest in carrying the matter further.

That Friday evening, in an appearance before Bristol University students, the Prime Minister acted as if he were enjoying all the fuss. To the sounds of loud cheering, he agreed that perhaps he was in "a bit of a scrape."[15] The implication was, however, that the whole thing was really a tempest in a tea cup.

A few days later the Prime Minister confided to a close friend that he was worried because the Montgomery telegram was definitely not in his book and he could not locate it anywhere.[16] It may or may not have been to Churchill's advantage that during the critical period following his Woodford revelation the House of Commons was preparing for a brief recess. This five-day interval allowed for considerable airing of the speech in the daily press and extensive commentary. It was clear that when Parliament reconvened, the matter could not be ignored. Although Churchill was to win an extra day—his birthday fête—no time was wasted at the December 1 meeting to start the cross-examination.

The probing was begun by a Labor M.P. from Easington, who, with vast understatement, requested permission to direct House attention to the Prime Minister's speech of the 23rd of November. Although extending his apologies for opening such a controversy in the aftermath of birthday celebrations, the Labor M.P., Mr. Emmanuel Shinwell, alleged as to how there was "considerable excitement, confusion and bewilderment in the public mind."[17]

Urged on by the Prime Minister to do his duty, Shinwell launched into his subject with evident relish. He reviewed the remarks that Sir Winston had reportedly made at Woodford, interspersing questions from time to time. He asked, for example, had the Prime Minister actually sent such a message and did he really seriously consider rearming German troops to fight Russia? It was now apparent, Shinwell continued, that no such message to Montgomery or Eisenhower appeared in Churchill's published works, and while those messages that did appear warning of Communist dangers proved quite valid, they were a far cry from any direct order to ready the German army to fight the Soviets.[18] With this statement, several Honorable Members asked, "With German troops?" To which Mr. Churchill replied, "Of course, if they went on."[19]

Continuing, Shinwell now described the published telegrams that were sent to Eisenhower, Truman and Eden—all after the war

in Europe was over—containing references to preserving German
military equipment, but no mention of the use of German soldiers
to fight Russia. He reminded House members not to forget that at
the very time Churchill allegedly sent his telegram to Montgomery,
the Western Allies were busily preparing for a conference (Potsdam) of peace with the Soviet Union. The Laborite asked why
Churchill did not address his orders to Eisenhower, then Supreme
Commander of Allied Forces, instead of to Montgomery? Why had
the Prime Minister omitted this very important detail from his
World War Two history? Why and for what purpose did he now
reveal it?[20]

Mr. Shinwell wondered aloud if it was possible that the message
was never sent, to which Churchill nodded assent, however, Shinwell said there must have been some basis for it all even if the
Prime Minister had become confused somewhere. "Did he intend
to continue the war? Imagine the effect on the troops, on the
gallant remnants of the Desert Rats who were fighting in Normandy at the end of the war, if they had been asked, having
destroyed Rommel and his forces, to be associated with the Nazi
German troops against our former allies."[21]

Pursuing this line, Shinwell expressed some puzzlement that
amidst the current excitement there had been no wounded out-
burst from the Soviet Union except for a brief *Pravda* comment.
Was it just possible, Shinwell asked, that the Soviets knew what
Churchill was up to? "They might have known," he said, "and if
they knew that we were prepared to associate with the Nazi forces
at that time and to avail ourselves of their support, the knowledge
might have soured their policy and outlook ever since."[22]

(Marshal Zhukov claimed that Soviet authorities received
knowledge of Churchill's telegram shortly after war's end. Quoting
what he called a "secret cable" sent to Montgomery by the British
leader "during the final campaign in the West," the Soviet Marshal
provided the gist of the description given by Churchill at
Woodford.)[23]

It was now time for the old Prime Minister to speak in his own
defense and he began with the disarming technique of admitting
that possibly he had made a mistake. He said that he really
believed, when speaking at Woodford, that he had sent the telegram to Montgomery and that it was also published in his account

of World War II. The Prime Minister conceded that the entire affair could have been avoided if he had taken the care to check his sources, a piece of advice so often given to others. He had been searching for it, he said, but no trace could be found. However, when Montgomery returned from America on the fourth of the month, the Field Marshal would search his own records too. In preparing his listeners for disappointment, Churchill hinted strongly that he might well have been confused about the whole thing after all.[24]

However, for one who confessed to some confusion, Churchill used rather precise language at times in his discussion, for he clearly remembered that no "Cabinet assent was sought for this particular telegram. It was only of a precautionary character, and, if it were sent at all, it went only as one of scores of similar messages which were passing at the time about the German surrender."[25] He told his listeners that he distinctly and strongly felt that victory could have become tragedy in 1945, and did not conceal those feelings of deep apprehension, for the "situation which we faced in May 1945, was . . . threatening."[26] In fact, he said, even if the telegram had never existed, it was just what he had been thinking anyway:

> As we had in Montgomery's theatre alone more than a million disarmed German prisoners of war who had surrendered to us—to us, I say, I felt we were responsible for taking measures for their protection, and if we were unable to carry out our terms of capitulation or to afford them that protection for which we were responsible, it might become a matter of honour as well as policy to give them back their arms.[27]

The Prime Minister went on to explain that all of this contemplated action hinged upon a Soviet advance westward. Therefore, he felt that Russia should be warned "that we should certainly in that case rearm German prisoners in our hands, who already, including those in Italy, numbered two and a half million."[28] Continuing, he observed that even in 1945, he did not judge the German army as others did by their "political label. I think that the majority were ordinary people compelled into military service and fighting desperately in defense of their native land. . . . That is where I stood at the moment of victory in the first part of May 1945." In closing, he formally expressed his regret at the affair—

calling attention to the rarity of such expression—but insisted that it was not a speech made on the "spur of the moment."[29]

Strangely, no more questions were forthcoming from House members and a motion was made to accept both Churchill's explanation and apology, such as they were. It should not be forgotten, in attempting to understand the mood of the House at this point, that the year 1954 was already deep into the Cold War controversy, and both the United States and Great Britain were extensively engaged in efforts to erect a European Defense Community as a bulwark against the expansion of communism. The Woodford episode was, therefore, unfolding in an atmosphere dramatically different from that of 1945, and many people large and small heartily endorsed the remarks of the old pugnacious statesman.

An additional reason for the mild House reaction, at least for the moment, was supplied by Lord Moran, who wrote that the House Speaker personally told him that many members were totally disarmed by Churchill's uncharacteristic behavior in confessing the error of his ways and expected matters to now calm down. Churchill provided the good doctor with his own version: "I made a goose of myself at Woodford, forgetting what I'd done."[30]

On the following day, December 2, two very brief written questions were submitted to the Prime Minister in regard to possible terms arrived at between Field Marshal Montgomery and Field Marshal von Busch, and if he intended to reveal any preparations made for the use of German troops against Soviet forces.[31] The thrust of the inquiries indicated doubt by a persistent few that was not totally dispelled by Sir Winston's famous candor. The Prime Minister was becoming increasingly impatient with the questioning, however, and simply refused to elaborate on his remarks of the previous day.[32]

Not so willing to buy a poor story, the press awaited Montgomery's arrival on the fourth with much fanfare, hopeful that some new information would be provided. Montgomery, however, was equally as reticent as his Prime Minister with the reporters who besieged him at the airport. He firmly stated that he intended to spend the weekend—it was Saturday—searching at home for the now famous telegram and would inform Churchill of the results.

Asked directly if he had the telegram in his personal files, Montgomery replied, "I can not say. I did receive a message; that is a
fact. I said it in the United States; I say it again, I did receive
it."[3] A fairly positive response by any standards!

If Parliament had been inclined to forget and forgive on Friday,
Montgomery's Saturday statement destroyed all such thinking,
and although Churchill let it be known that he would soon publish
all relevant information, he did not succeed in heading off the
attack.[34] By midweek, the barrage began with specific requests on
the exact wording of the instructions sent to Montgomery in May
1945, and an explanation of the nature of preparations made for
the actual use of German troops. In addition, the reminder was
given that no satisfactory answer had been given to the question of
the previous week, namely, the nature of the arrangements made
between Montgomery and his German counterpart, von Busch.
Churchill answered that he had not yet located the message and
thus, could not provide exact wording; secondly, German troops
were not held in readiness after surrender; and thirdly, no arrangements were made by Montgomery with Busch.[35]

When this approach failed to crack Churchill's armor, a new
tack was tried and Churchill was asked if he was aware of the
profound shock that his revelation had caused among people
everywhere? Sir Winston answered that he did not know about
this, but "of course, some people are very hard up to find
something to talk about."[36] His good friend Lord Moran was of
like mind, noting that the "country doesn't seem interested; it is
certainly not indignant."[37]

Churchill must have known better than this, for the facts were
that a major figure of his time had—either purposely or inadver-
tently—disclosed a monumental wartime secret so closely guarded
that by all evidence, it appeared that not even the Supreme Allied
Commander knew of it. Surely, it was highly naive of Churchill to
expect people not to talk about this disclosure.

Support in favor of the Prime Minister's stand was offered from
notable figures such as Sir Hartley Shawcross, who declared that
he failed to understand the furor since the danger of a Russian
advance in 1945 was feared by all: "If that had happened," the
famed jurist commented, "we would have had to resist it by all
available means. That might have included the use of Germans

under Allied command."[38] If the possibility of a Russian advance westward was common knowledge, as Shawcross maintained, it is curious that virtually no mention of it has been found in contemporary records and memoirs. Clearly, there is a vast difference between a growing recognition of the Russian menace in 1945, and a certain knowledge that Stalin planned to continue his push westward unless challenged.

Deviating from this theme for the moment, House members chose to explore the question of Montgomery's authority, or possible lack thereof, to retain military records after his army career had seemingly ended. The point came up when the Prime Minister was asked, facetiously no doubt, if he planned to bring proceedings against the Field Marshal (under the Official Secrets Act) for violating declaration C of Appendix XXX to Queen's Regulations in which he had stated that he possessed no records not authorized by his superior officer. Churchill immediately answered with a resounding no, pointing out that Montgomery had not left the army, and presumably had signed no such regulation. In fact, he said, everyone should know that a Field Marshal is never retired and holds rank for life.[39]

Fastening now on a vital issue that could prove a way out, the Prime Minister carefully explained that he had been diligently searching for the lost telegram, exhausting every possible avenue for information and leads, when he became aware that all top secret messages sent to commanders at the front "were, by order, destroyed immediately when they had been orally imparted." This bit of news caused Laborite William Ross to remark, "That explains the telegram." Ignoring the interruption, Churchill continued that it was obvious that large numbers of very secret messages were dispatched to the front ("Altogether, I find that from the 1st of January to . . . end of July, I received or sent 1,250 personal and private telegrams of the most secret character"), and subsequently destroyed in the field. He left the distinct impression that he believed this to have been the fate of his telegram to Montgomery.[40] A few additional attempts were made to pin down Montgomery's exact status accompanied by veiled hints that the Field Marshal was not above the law. However, the session had become hopelessly lost in points of order and nothing more was accomplished on the subject at hand.[41]

Debate was resumed on December 14, with House members recalling that in the period of the German offensive in the Ardennes (1944-45), Churchill requested and received from Stalin an intensified Russian attack upon German forces on the Eastern front. One member asked, "Is the Prime Minister not aware that hundreds of thousands of young Russians lost their lives, and that a few months afterwards he was prepared to build up the German military machine again?" Churchill's angry retort was, "Hundreds of thousands of young Britons lost their lives in the first two years of the war when the Russians were in league with Hitler."[42]

It was obvious that, as the days passed, many House members had been doing their homework and exploring side issues on their own. One such member asked the Prime Minister if he was aware of a very similar message having been sent to Allied Headquarters in Italy, about the same time as the alleged telegram had gone to Montgomery in 1945? Churchill agreed that the warning to stack German weapons might very well have been sent to both Field Marshals (Montgomery and Alexander) routinely. The House member, Mr. Lewis, revealed that an ex-army captain had been located who had been senior cypher officer at Allied Headquarters in Italy and had decoded the very message in question. Before this fact could be pursued, Churchill offered the observation that that time had been filled with pressures and confusion and "a lot was going on."[43]

The Prime Minister may have been thinking of the additional threat of Communist advance that he saw in the Balkans as well as the Baltic. The papers of Field Marshal Alexander[44] do contain messages from Churchill during that early May period of 1945, with language very similar to the reported Montgomery message. The possible danger that Alexander faced was resistance to British military policy in Yugoslavia from the forces of Tito, who in turn had Soviet support. On May 5, Alexander had notified the Prime Minister that an extremely tense situation had developed and that the Yugoslav partisan leader flatly refused to withdraw his forces before the British. Alexander cautioned that "we must bear in mind that since our last meeting he has been in Moscow." Immediately, the Prime Minister replied, "Let me know what you are doing in massing forces against this Moscovite tentacle, of which Tito is the crook."[45]

Churchill's inclination was to send Tito a strongly worded warning against any attack on the British troops, however, Alexander thought this would not help. He told the Prime Minister, "I am sure our soldiers will obey orders, but I doubt that they will re-enter battle, this time against the Yugoslavs, with the same enthusiasm as they did against the hated Germans."[46]

In the parliamentary discussions of 1954, this exchange between Churchill and Alexander was not revealed. When asked specifically about official telegrams sent to commanders at the front that were open to official historians, the Prime Minister stated that none "of the telegrams available in our London records have been withheld from the official historians."[47]

The last public exchange that occurred on the Woodford affair came on December 14, and ended with a few brief written questions directed to the Prime Minister concerning any current discussion he might have had with Field Marshal Montgomery about the telegram; whether it had been located; and whether he intended to publish the contents in *Hansard*. Churchill's final public comments were equally brief. He stated that he had made his position clear on the subject on December 7, and that the situation remained unchanged. He flatly refused to reveal any of the content of discussions with Montgomery, or any one else for that matter, ending all further debate by indignantly saying, "I cannot recall any precedent for such demands among Members of Parliament."[48] Thus ended the Woodford incident.

The major purpose here is to suggest that a primary cause of the Cold War is to be found in the record of enmity and disagreements between Great Britain and the Soviet Union, which began to reach crisis proportions in 1943 and almost erupted into a third world war in May of 1945.

Germany, a nation in the throes of disintegration, grasping for any thread of survival, was the potential force that Winston Churchill planned to take as a partner in his efforts to stop Soviet armies from moving into northwestern Europe. Weeks and months after the Second World War in Europe had officially ended and Churchill was no longer the Prime Minister, Soviet Russia continued to charge Great Britain with keeping a large German army in a state of preparedness. These charges were generally accompanied by details of names, places, and units in training in the British zone of occupation.

When a renowned leader of the Western world spoke as Winston Churchill did to his people at Woodford, affording a small glimpse into his wartime thought and action, it must be taken seriously. By 1954, when Churchill made his comments, the Cold War had greatly deepened and taken on its familiar theme of Russia versus the United States, but it was still possible to see the outlines of an earlier struggle in which the chief antagonists had been Great Britain and Russia.

The history of differences between the two nations since the Bolshevik victory of 1917, is lengthy and the relationship has seldom been smooth, although circumstances occasionally produced periods of lesser hostility, and in fact, a mood almost verging on toleration would temporarily surface. Such periods came in the 1920s and 1930s; however, with the rise to power of Mussolini and Hitler, a new threat appeared. The emergence of the Fascist states caused some Englishmen to take a more benevolent view of the Soviet Union. Many Britishers, however, adopted the exact opposite view and began to feel that the Fascists offered the best bulwark against communism. These opinions, combined with a pronounced national desire to avoid future conflicts at all costs, made the taking of sides in foreign policy the burning issues as the prewar decade drew to a close.

When the war began in September 1939, the mutual Russo-English hostilities had already reached the point of no return with the Munich Agreement and the Molotov-Ribbentrop Pact. The German attack on Russia in 1941 appeared to reverse much of this history, however, and the next two years were largely buried in the battle to defeat Hitler. Many people forgot that war breeds strange bedfellows, and that the British-Soviet understanding was a temporary condition. In fact, it did not even survive the war.

In 1943, there were already Allied speculations about using Hitler's war machine to help halt a possible Russian advance into Europe, but all evidence indicates that the crucial step from speculation to action was made by Great Britain and not the United States. Just why the United States, or more accurately, some of its wartime leaders, seemed more concerned about Russian expansion into Europe in 1943 than in 1945 is difficult to say. The huge growth in America's power during that interval must be considered as one major reason.

All this meant that Churchill's anxieties about having to face the Russians alone were founded in reality, and that no doubt these anxieties prompted him to take the first measures to try and stop the Communist advance before the war had ended. It is very important to take note of the fact that even after Churchill had turned over his office to Laborite Clement Attlee, attempts to maintain German forces in British hands continued. These actions were very definitely related to escalating tensions between Great Britain and the Soviet Union in 1945-46, and became identifiable with the policies of the United States by 1947. Although by that time the German wartime forces had been disbanded, military and political leaders of the Western world spoke openly of the need for a new force, and it was a public secret that many statesmen deplored the loss of the German army.

NOTES

1. R. Churchill, ed., *The Unwritten Alliance: Speeches 1953 to 1959 by Winston S. Churchill* (London: Cassell, 1961), pp. 196-97.

2. Loc. cit.

3. C. Moran, *Churchill: Taken from the Diaries of Lord Moran* (Boston: Houghton Mifflin, 1966), pp. 648-49.

4. New York *Times*, November 24, 1954.

5. *The Times* (London), November 25, 1954. Several years later, when Montgomery's memoirs were published, very little had been added to throw any light on the incident. The Field Marshal made somewhat vague references to "formations . . . kept by me as reserve in case trouble developed. I had also been given a 'stand still' order regarding the destruction of German weapons and equipment, in case they might be needed by the Western Allies for any reason." *The Memoirs of Field Marshal, The Viscount Montgomery* (New York: World Publishing Co., 1958), p. 321.

6. *The Times* (London), November 25, 1954.

7. Loc. cit

8. Ibid., November 27, 1954.

9. *Heidelberger Tageblatt*, November 26, 1954.

10. *Rhein-Neckar Zeitung*, November 25, 1954.

11. *Neue Rhein Zeitung*, November 26, 1954.

12. A New York *Times* article mentioned the telegram on November 26, 1954.

13. *Triumph and Tragedy* (Boston: Houghton Mifflin, 1953), pp. 499 and 469.

14. *The Times* (London), November 26, 1954.

15. Ibid., November 27, 1954.

16. Moran, *Churchill*, pp. 651-52. Moran noted that a vain search for the very same telegram had been made three years previously by one of the persons aiding Churchill in his research. The conclusion had been then that the P.M. "must have decided at the last moment not to send it." Ibid., p. 652.

17. *House of Commons Debates*, 5th Series, Vol. 535 (1954-55), pp. 149-60.

18. Ibid., pp. 161-63.

19. Ibid., p. 163

20. Ibid., pp. 163-64.

21. Ibid., pp. 166-67.

22. Loc. cit.

23. G. Zhukov, *The Memoirs of Marshal Zhukov* (London: Delacorte, 1971), p. 665.

24. *House of Commons Debates*, 5th Series, Vol. 535 (1954-55), pp. 170-71.

25. Loc. cit.

26. Ibid., p. 172.

27. Ibid., pp. 173-74.

28. Loc. cit.

29. Ibid., p. 176.

30. Moran, *Churchill*, p. 657.

31. *House of Commons Debates*, 5th Series, Vol. 535 (1954-55), p. 7.

32. Loc. cit.

33. *The Times* (London), December 6, 1954.

34. *House of Commons Debates*, 5th Series, Vol. 535 (1954-55), p. 602.

35. Ibid., pp. 771-72.

36. Ibid., pp. 772-73

37. Moran, *Churchill*, p. 661.

38. *The Times* (London), December 8, 1954.

39. *House of Commons Debates*, 5th Series, Vol. 535 (1954-55), pp. 1109-1111.

40. Ibid., p. 1112.

41. Ibid., pp. 1115-1116.

42. Ibid., p. 1574.

43. Ibid., p. 1575.

44. Great Britain, Public Records Office, War Office, 214/42, "Papers of Field Marshal Alexander," File No. 17, Vol. 111.

45. Ibid., Documents 21 through 26.

46. Ibid., Documents 27 through 32.

47. *House of Commons Debates*, 5th Series, Vol. 535 (1954-55), p. 1581.

48. Ibid., pp. 1579-1580.

Chapter 2

THE POLITICS OF STRATEGY, 1943

Sometime during the year of 1943, Allied leaders began to think seriously about the possible consequences of a Russian victory over Germany. The year was decisive in several ways. The war was at midpoint and the Axis powers were moving from offense to defense. Unfortunately for the Western planners, this conclusion had to be drawn from the Russian victory at Stalingrad rather than an Allied invasion of the Continent. The specter of a Russian-occupied Europe while Allied might was still assembling in England was a sobering thought indeed.

Looking back on these events, a War Department historian wistfully acknowledged, in 1948, that "Perhaps we should have changed our policy after the Soviet victory at Stalingrad and the first effective Soviet counteroffensive in early 1943. By coming to terms with the Germans, if not the Nazis, we could conceivably have employed their manpower and industrial resources in containing the Soviet Union."[1]

If the time and events are considered in light of such an analysis, there were obvious attractions on both sides (Russia and the Western Allies) to a German peace in 1943. Certain facts were plain: an Allied invasion was a year away, and the Soviets were already advancing westward. If Germany collapsed suddenly—which seemed a real possibility that year—the Russians would be into central and western Europe before the Allies. The great planned invasion of the Continent would have remained just a plan, and the Soviet Union would stand before the world as the nation that defeated Hitler. No amount of discussion could have changed this and the immense prestige that would have gone with it in influencing the entire course of history for postwar Europe.

Such thoughts must have been frequent companions for Western statesmen and military leaders in the spring of 1943. Under the circumstances, it is not surprising that many people gave serious consideration to possible alternatives. Actually, there seemed to be only two real working possibilities for stopping the Russian advance, and both of them entailed the most drastic of measures for any chance of success.

The two choices were (1) to make a separate peace with Hitler and allow the Germans to continue the war in the East against Russia; and (2) in the event of a German collapse, to incorporate the armed might of Hitler's armies into the Allied command and force the Russians to stand fast in eastern Europe.

To many people in the West, a separate peace was the more appealing for several reasons. As Hanson Baldwin wrote, "it would have been to the interest of Britain, the United States and the world to have allowed—and indeed encouraged—the world's two great dictatorships to fight each other to a frazzle," for we did not need Russia, she needed us. "In retrospect, how stupid we were!"[2]

Of course, the possibilities that they might be suddenly confronted with a shifting alliance were not lost upon the Soviets either. In the summer of 1943, Stalin openly expressed concern over the surrender of Italy to the West without full Russian participation. What was on his mind was not very hard to guess; as one Soviet journalist asked, "Did this [Italian negotiations] mean that London and Washington would deal with Goering when the time came?"[3] Soviet Marshal I. S. Konev suggested that the most likely choice for the Western Allies was a German surrender in the West and a continuance of the war against Russia; "we had absolutely no right to preclude that contingency."[4]

Keeping events in perspective, it should not be forgotten that from 1938 to 1943 is only a brief five-year span, and the memory of 1938 was very much in people's minds: "I was always aware of the fact that Munich with all of its catastrophic European consequences would not have occurred," the Czech leader Eduard Beneš wrote, "but for the hostility of Western Europe towards the Soviet Union."[5]

Specifically, Beneš regarded it a major part of his responsibility in that fateful year of 1943 to try to establish sufficient harmony between the West and Stalin to preclude any chance of Hitler securing a free hand on the eastern front. Beneš soon had to admit that his self-appointed mission met with very limited success, for while "in Washington I found full understanding . . . in London the situation was somewhat different." He was forced to the gloomy conclusion that the Germans, knowing full well the delicacy of East-West differences, would soon begin an intense anti-Bolshevik campaign aimed at the Western world and, unfortunately, find receptive ears in Washington and London.[6]

Not missing a trick, the Nazis aimed their barrage in the westerly direction just as Beneš predicted, but at the same time properly evaluated the Russians as the far more realistic partner in peace. Ironically, this thought was held by some of the leaders of the German opposition to Hitler, too.[7]

Predictably, the world's embassies and consulates became hotbeds of unsubstantiated reports and rumors of separate peace activity. An American diplomatic message out of Finland in early 1943 reported the German Foreign Minister Ribbentrop in the role of an activist seeking immediate compromise with Russia. Similar information came from other posts in Switzerland and Spain, supposedly based on the most reliable of sources and placing Ribbentrop in Moscow already.[8]

Joachim von Ribbentrop, elevated to Foreign Ministry head in 1938 and a devout Hitler follower, had suggested as early as 1942 that some agreement with Moscow should be explored. After the Fuehrer had angrily rejected any such possibility, the Nazi Minister allowed some time to elapse before he broached the matter again. He decided that the imminent collapse of Italy provided a reasonable opportunity to reopen the question and during the spring of 1943 requested permission to arrange a meeting with Stalin.[9] Although rebuffed by Hitler a second time, Ribbentrop continued to occupy a key role in these early peace speculations. It is a matter of record that he had already submitted a plan to Hitler on the subject after the Allied landing in North Africa in November 1942, and that despite risking the Fuehrer's wrath, he had persisted in his efforts. In 1943, Ribbentrop had gained a powerful supporter in Benito Mussolini; and the Italian dictator discussed the idea with Hitler at a spring meeting in Austria. Again, the Fuehrer turned down the advice.[10]

It is almost unthinkable that Ribbentrop could have arranged a meeting with the Soviets in midwar without the knowledge of the Western Allies, and yet, a most highly respected military historian, Basil Lidell-Hart, has written that "according to German officers who attended as technical advisers, Ribbentrop [behind the German lines at Kirovograd in June 1943] proposed as a condition of peace that Russia's future frontier should run along the Dnieper, while Molotov would not consider anything less than the restoration of her original frontier."[11] Unfortunately, Lidell-Hart has left no documentation for his astounding claim. It can almost be assumed that if such a meeting had occurred, Ribbentrop would have mentioned it at Nuremberg unless prevented from doing so, which seems highly unlikely.

Moving to more solid ground, there is another dimension of Ribbentrop's separate peace effort that is not quite as elusive as the questionable meeting on the eastern front. This particular aspect of the separate peace puzzle began at approximately the same period as the alleged preliminaries for a Ribbentrop-Molotov meeting. A German contact of Ribbentrop's, Peter Kleist, was approached by a Russian agent while in Stockholm in June 1943. By Kleist's own account, he was accosted in the Swedish capital on the 18th by a man named Clauss who boasted of close association with the top Russian leadership. Among other things, Clauss reportedly complained about the delay of a second front while the Western Allies appeared content to place the war burden on Russian shoulders.[12]

When informed of the encounter, Ribbentrop's first reaction was skeptical but interested. According to Kleist, the Foreign Minister knew only too well that Hitler's attitude was absolutely negative, but asked to be kept informed of any further contacts.

Kleist interpreted this to mean that while Ribbentrop would not make it a specific assignment, he was definitely for unofficial continuance of the Stockholm venture.[13]

Some time later, Kleist was told by his Stockholm informant that he had been judged acceptable for conducting the preliminary discussions. The information was dropped that Soviet demands would probably include a restoration of her 1914 borders. Kleist dutifully passed this intelligence on, but too much time had elapsed and by all appearances the Russians did not have to bargain any more.[14] Interestingly, this was exactly the conclusion arrived at by Western military leadership at about the same time.[15]

The German case was not helped by the fact that the Soviets had information that Germany was preparing to make use of captured Russian troops under General Andrei Vlasov on the eastern front.[16]

While intrigue and rumor made an accurate evaluation almost impossible for the Western powers, there was sufficient information to take the possibility of a Russo-German peace with all seriousness. This meant pushing ahead with the utmost speed on second front planning and preparations. Meanwhile, the idea that Russia could be tied to the West in some manner that would preclude any agreement with the Germans emerged with the unconditional surrender formula.

The unconditional surrender announcement was made by President Franklin Roosevelt on January 23, 1943 at the Casablanca Conference. Lord Hankey, a member of Churchill's administration, wrote that "at noon on the next day, Sunday . . . less than twenty-four hours after he had propounded the idea, the President, apparently without further warning to Mr. Churchill, announced it to the Press of the world assembled in the garden of the villa where he and Mr. Churchill were seated side by side in the warm African sunshine."[17]

The Times (London) reported that the American President had explained to newsmen that the phrase had been inspired by the American General U. S. Grant.[18] Roosevelt added that he did not mean that this was a policy of destruction aimed at the populations of the enemy countries, but at their leadership. In concluding, the two statesmen agreed that the meeting might well be called the "Unconditional Surrender Meeting," and "Mr. Churchill . . . repeated . . . the phrase that Mr. Roosevelt has put in so memorable a setting."[19]

Of course, there is evidence to strongly suggest that Mr. Roosevelt's "phrase" was neither spontaneous nor original, for Churchill admitted having discussed the same subject using the very words "unconditional surrender" with his war cabinet on the previous January 20th.[20] The importance, however, lay not in the credit due column, but obviously in the impact of the announcement itself.

The unconditional surrender policy soon became embroiled in controversy. The difficulty was in deciding whether the positive features outweighed the negative ones. Its obvious and immediate merits were propaganda value and a general strengthening of Allied resolve, hopefully to be endorsed by Stalin, that the Germans would face a far different situation than that of November 1918, and on the face of it, there did not seem to be any thing wrong with letting the enemy know that there would be no easy way out.

In an interesting twist of meaning, the German opposition to Hitler regarded the unconditional surrender announcement with favor, for the opposition leaders decided that it showed the Allies wanted to save Western culture and keep the Red Army out of Germany.[21] In part this perverted interpretation stemmed from the existence of the Russian-sponsored "Free Germany Movement," for after Stalingrad this National Committee to Free Germany represented a potentially powerful propaganda instrument. While there was no doubt that the organization served at Russia's convenience, the possibility that Hitler might be overthrown gave the group a chance of participating in peace negotiations. Pursuing this line of thinking, the German home opposition could also rejoice at the unconditional surrender because that would preclude any early armistice with the Soviets—providing Stalin agreed to it.[22]

Of course, Nazi Propaganda Minister Joseph Goebbels turned the statement into a powerful argument for greater effort on the German home front and a fight to the death by soldiers in the field. An American official in the Office of Wartime Information (OWI) observed that, "A few months after Casablanca it became clear from analysis of enemy propaganda as well as from prisoner interrogation that the 'unconditional surrender' formula was back-firing against us."[2 3]

There was still a possibility for the Western Allies to seize the initiative again by mounting a massive propaganda campaign to convince the German people that they were not the targets for destruction and that early surrender would prove it. To launch such a program meant that some additional clarification had to come from the very highest level, preferably Roosevelt himself. A statement meant to provide a clear "Policy Toward the German People" was drafted by the OWI for the American President's consideration in May 1943, offering those Germans who did not support Hitler's regime some hope for a way out. The statement was returned, however, with no action taken, and subsequent Allied meetings only reaffirmed the original policy. Later, when an appropriate clarification was finally provided by Roosevelt, it was too late for the damage had been done.[2 4]

The immediate losers were the people in the American Psychological Warfare Division (PWD or "Sykewar"), for now the power to promise had suddenly vanished. They made every attempt to regain the advantage by hammering at the fact that the object of Allied force was the German army and not the civilian population, but there is little evidence that this had much impact.[2 5]

Postwar works by former German military leaders explored the question of the influence of the unconditional surrender demand at Casablanca. One source reports a conversation on the subject between General von Falkenhausen and Field Marshal von Kluge in Paris in June of 1944. Falkenhausen said the German situation was hopeless unless negotiations could be opened with the Allies while at the same time action was undertaken on the home front against Hitler. Von Kluge answered, "Absolutely, if it were not for the 'unconditional surrender!' "[2 6]

It is true that the unconditional surrender served the purpose of "reassuring the Russians, that in spite of necessary delays over the opening of the second front, it was still the Western determination to press on . . . as soon as the physical forces could be assembled to do the job."[2 7]   And, while the Russians had heard all of this before, they had to be satisfied with the hope of a promise fulfilled.

A point of considerable significance here was the past difference between the United States and Great Britain over the date of opening a second front. In fact, the view that the West should not launch an invasion of the Continent until some future date when greater strength was attained was powerfully championed by Winston Churchill. The stand taken by the United States was best expressed by the American Chief of Staff, General George C. Marshall, who backed the plan for a full-scale landing in France in 1942, which proved completely unfeasible, but did illustrate American impatience with any delay. The disagreement ran deep and was not a very well-kept secret.[28] Stalin became aware of the opposing views and grew increasingly hostile toward the British.[29]

The opinion has been expressed that by his demand for a second front in 1941-42, when it was virtually an impossibility, Stalin provided Churchill with "a ready means of discrediting such impossible requests. . . . There is little doubt the Soviet dictator must have considered British inaction on the Continent, even in 1941, as deliberate."[30]

In May 1942, Russia's Foreign Minister Molotov visited President Roosevelt in Washington, and was assured that his government "could expect a second front this year."[31] Closer examination reveals, so goes one line of reasoning, that "could expect" did not mean absolutely; it meant that every sincere effort would be made to bring about an invasion in 1942, hopefully in October.[32]

Stalin was understandably bitter about it,[33] but the possibility that the Soviet leaders did not really take the American President's promise all that seriously has been suggested: "It is far more likely that the Russians were reacting to prewar suggestions in the British and American press and in Parliament and Congress that Germany and the U.S.S.R. be allowed to destroy each other."[34]

Fuel was thrown on the fire by public figures like Wendell Wilkie, who, while visiting Moscow in September 1942, suggested that both U.S. and British leaders needed "public prodding" to open a second front, and it was no secret that he placed the major share of the blame on the British for the delay.[35]

By October, the news from Moscow was openly critical with reference to the influence in Great Britain of the "Clivedon Set" and Lady Astor, as well as "favored" treatment being given to

Rudolf Hess. Generally, the "Second Front delays were strength-ening the fundamental dislike for the Western Powers that so many had felt for the last twenty-five years."[36] An examination of the Soviet press and literature at that specific time reveals a general outpouring of accusations against the Allies for the delay, although the more bitter charges were reserved for the British. This prompted one British general, Frederick Morgan, to remark that although he was favorable toward the American viewpoint, still "the taunting from the Kremlin . . . [was] already becoming more than a little annoying."[37]

With the constant specter of a separate peace lurking in the background and no immediate prospects of a second front, the state of the Russo-Allied relationship began to reach an ebb by the summer of 1943. Added to Allied concern was the growing convic-tion that Germany might collapse at any moment, allowing the Russians to flow into the vacuum before the West could arrive in force. The possibility of a Soviet-held Europe while the Western Allies were still gathering forces in England for the invasion seemed to grow more real from day to day.

In an attempt to meet all possible contingencies, the Allied had already decided to prepare for both a quick entry into Germany in case of an unexpected collapse and at the same time continue preparations for the full-scale European invasion in 1944. The 1944 invasion plan, codenamed OVERLORD, began with the certainty of a fixed date toward which the planning staffs could work, but the same was not true for the other phase, which included many intangibles.

This portion, called RANKIN (successor to SLEDGEHAMMER and ROUNDUP), was under the direction of General Frederick Morgan, who had been entrusted with the task in April of 1943. From the outset, the difficulties of planning for RANKIN were obvious. Unable at first to get a clear idea of what the Allied Chiefs of Staff meant by a German collapse, Morgan decided the best course to aim for was someplace between invasion and total collapse, but not to rule out any variety of situations in between.[38]

This proved far more difficult than it sounded and there was still no plan by July. Morgan was still searching for some working definition of collapse and at the same time deciding how the occupation was to be organized if Germany fell quickly. Morgan wrote that "it was difficult to find anyone who had begun to think realistically on any of these subjects."[39]

Finally, RANKIN was drawn for three possibilities: (a) sending forces through a weakened German defense; (b) meeting German withdrawal from certain areas; and (c) a complete collapse as happened in 1918. The last, designated RANKIN C, had already started on the subject of "Post Hostilities Planning," but little had been accomplished. It was just assumed that as Germany disintegrated, the British would occupy the northwest, the Americans the southwest, and the Russians the east. However, this had not yet been developed with any exactitude and no decisions arrived at on definite boundaries. Questions on just how Germany was to be governed, how many administrations, and how to dispose of Berlin, were not worked out completely. A suggestion that each occupied area be governed by the three victors was considered, although the Russians were not included in the planning stage at all.[40] This was the general situation when the first Quebec Conference neared in August and the Allies gathered to consider their problems. Specifically, it was in this atmosphere that the American Chief of Staff, General George C. Marshall, voiced his concern about Soviet intentions.

On August 20, the British Chief of Staff, Sir Alan Brooke, reviewed the Russian military position and concluded that it was strong and growing more so. He thought the chance of Germany gaining a negotiated peace with the Russians was very unlikely. After mention of the formation of the "Free Germany" movement (German prisoners-of-war in Russia pledged to aid anti-Nazi propaganda efforts), General Marshall referred to reports he had recently received that indicated growing hostility in Russia toward the West. In fact, Marshall felt that the Soviets were actually "becoming increasingly contemptuous. Their recent 'Second Front' announcement no longer born of despair, was indicative of this attitude." Marshall continued that he "would be interested to know the British Chiefs of Staff's view on the possible results of the situation in Russia with regard to the deployment of Allied forces—for example, in the event of an overwhelming Russian success, would the Germans be likely to facilitate our entry into the country to repel the Russians?"[41]

Sir Alan Brooke admitted that he too felt concerned about the opportunity that may be opened to the Russians by the chaos of war's end to advance communism. As a matter of fact, the British Chief said he had explored that very question with exiled Czech President Eduard Beneš, whose "view had been that since Russia would be terribly weakened after the war, she would require a period of recovery, and to speed up this recovery would require a peaceful Europe." All that would be necessary, Alan Brooke concluded, would be to concede to the Russian demands for a part of Poland, some of the Baltic states and Balkan concessions. "If she obtained these territories, she would be anxious to assist us in maintaining the peace of Europe."[42]

It is puzzling that Sir Alan Brooke seemed to place such high value on Beneš's judgment of a situation of the gravest concern to the Western Allies. Surely the Chiefs of Staff had extensive intelligence resources available to them for an evaluation that precluded such excessive reliance on an individual. While the Czech leader's loyalties did not appear to be in question, there was some doubt concerning his ability to handle Stalin. Clement Attlee's appraisal was: "Little Benes [sic] was quite sure he could fix everything, he only found out too late that he couldn't trust the Communists. . . . He was too clever by half."[43]

During the preceding May and June, 1943, President Beneš had made visits to Great Britain, Canada and the United States, where he met with both Churchill and Roosevelt at a White House conference. Although there is no official record of the meeting, Beneš wrote that the purpose of the meeting was to explain his views to the two Western leaders on the division of Germany and other matters pertaining thereto.[44] Beneš made no specific reference to any talk with Sir Alan Brooke at the time, although he was already certain that 1943 was the decisive year.[45]

He revealed that in a meeting in April with the Russians in Moscow he had been assured of their honorable intentions: "It [Russia] was determined to prosecute the war against Germany to the very end, but its detailed views on post-war Germany were greatly dependent on those of Great Britain and America."[46] Beneš did not conceal his opinion that the West definitely needed Russia to win the war, and that the Germans thought so too. Just as significant, he continued, was the fact that the struggle against

Germany was not merging into a well-coordinated effort by the Western Allies and their Russian partner. Beneš felt that the differences between the two camps were growing in direct proportion to the Soviet successes against Germany.[47]

Despite the growing tensions that surrounded the Quebec Conference, plans did proceed to approve Operation RANKIN, and General Morgan wrote that by the end of October 1943, RANKIN C had been issued as orders and directives to the First U.S. Army Group and the British 21st Army Group.[48] The American General Omar Bradley was to remark, however, that "by November . . . not an officer in London would have bet two shillings on the likelihood of German collapse. . . . RANKIN C was soon stuffed back into the files."[49]

Sometime between the Quebec Conference and the opening of the Teheran Conference at the end of November, the Allies began to detect signs that Stalin was not nearly as anxious for a second front as he had been the previous summer. General Marshall had already noted this at the Quebec meeting and later in October an even more noticeable shift was observed in the Soviet attitude: an apparent willingness to delay OVERLORD in deference to an immediate concentration on Italy.[50] With Stalingrad already being counted as a major Soviet victory, it was becoming increasingly obvious that Russian thinking had begun to weigh the distinct advantages of defeating the Nazis single-handedly as against the price of assistance that would come with a second front in the west.[51]

Clearly the fundamental differences between the Western Allies and the Soviet Union were growing more and more complex; however, planning for the pending Teheran Conference (November 28 through December 1) proceeded with the usual surface friendliness. A most revealing account of just how Stalin felt at the Conference was provided by the American diplomat Charles E. Bohlen. In a set of secret minutes taken at a tripartite dinner on November 29, Bohlen began by stating that the "most notable feature of the dinner was the attitude of Marshall Stalin toward the Prime Minister. Marshall Stalin lost no opportunity to get in a dig at Mr. Churchill. . . . Marshal Stalin strongly implied on several occasions that Mr. Churchill nursed a secret affection for Germany and desired to see a soft peace."[52] The Soviet leader also remarked that although the Russians were simple folk, it would be in error to think that they did not see the obvious, which Bohlen interpreted as Stalin's irritation with the British for their "attitude on the question of OVERLOAD."[53]

The next evening at a celebration for Winston Churchill's sixty-ninth birthday, Stalin renewed his arguments against the British. At first it was marked by a series of mutually flattering toasts, but when the occasion reached the British Army Chief of Staff, "Marshal Stalin stood with the others, but he held his glass in his hand, and . . . with a twinkle in his eye, said he regretted that Sir Alan was unfriendly to the Soviet Union, and adopted a grim and distrustful attitude toward the Russians."[54]

Before the evening ended, there was a further exchange between the Soviet Marshal and General Brooke, which Churchill attempted to soften by a bit of conciliatory humor.[55] The thoughts had been voiced, however, and the mutual mistrust—even dislike—had openly surfaced.

A long-time acquaintance of Winston Churchill recalled that the only time she ever remembered him as depressed was upon his return from the Teheran Conference. When asked what was wrong, Churchill, without burdening his guest with lectures on current events, said, "I realized at Teheran for the first time what a small nation we are. There I sat with the great Russian bear on one side of me, with paws outstretched . . . and on the other, the great American buffalo, and between the two sat the poor little British donkey, who was the only one of the three who knew the right way home."[56]

Britain's wartime Prime Minister was no doubt convinced that the "right way home" meant, as a first step, recognizing Russia as the problem and persuading Roosevelt of this. He had already given voice to some of these thoughts while en route to Teheran. "Germany is finished," Churchill said, "though it may take some time to clean up the mess. The real problem now is Russia. I *can't* get the Americans to see it."[57] Complaints against the Americans came from another quarter as well before the conference had ended. General Brooke was to confide to his diary that in addition to all other problems, he despaired "of getting our American

friends to have any strategic vision. Their drag on us has seriously
affected our Mediterranean strategy and the whole conduct of the
war."[58]

The earlier war years had been ones of supreme effort in
establishing a production base and mounting a war machine, and
now, although the end was not yet within sight, the conviction of
final victory was there. With this conviction firmly in mind,
increasing attention was directed toward postwar planning and this
meant that politics simply could not be ignored. Despite obvious
U.S. sentiments to delay political questions until the peace conference, the critical stance of British leadership no longer passed
unnoticed. The American President's son Elliot, as observer and
companion of his father at Teheran, wrote that when Churchill
argued for a Balkan invasion, it was "obvious to everyone" that he
was really trying to forestall any Soviet encroachment in the area:
"Stalin knew it, I knew it, everybody knew it." Later, his father
told him, "Trouble is, the P. M. is thinking too much of the
post-war, and where England will be. He's scared of letting the
Russians get too strong."[59]

The real stumbling block was a basic difference in attitude
between the Americans and the British. A consistent theme in
British postwar criticism was that the Americans lacked political
awareness of military strategy. Practice had established a long
history of cooperation between the British politician and the army
general. The empire-commonwealth experience had served to pro-
duce political-minded military leaders. To the British military, the
political consequences of any battle were of prime importance.
The military historian Hanson Baldwin had suggested more bluntly
that American strategists were "sound militarily, but weak
politically."[60] This was a view concurred in by numerous British
war participants such as General Leslie Hollis. As a senior British
officer, he was in attendance at many of the wartime conferences
and placed much of the blame for American political ignorance
upon Roosevelt; at the same time heaping praise on the Prime
Minister for his very astute judgments about Stalin's intentions.
Hollis especially deplored the presence of Roosevelt's "clique of
faithful supporters—General Marshall, Ambassador Joseph Davies,
Harry Hopkins, and his own son Elliot—[who] missed no opportunity to praise the Soviet Union, in and out of season."[61]

Of course, much of this criticism, hidden in wartime propaganda, has long since become public, and to provide documentation becomes a task of selection. However, the point must be made that Churchill and people in his government were becoming embarrassingly aware by 1943 of their limitations in trying to shape the postwar world. Since 1941, the United States and Russia were the prime reasons for Hitler's significant weakening; without American production and Russia's absorption of German military might in the east, Great Britain might well have been a part of Nazi-occupied Europe by 1943.

No one knew better than Winston Churchill that his beloved England might well face an even more serious battle at war's end than she had in 1940. The rules of the game had changed and so had the players: the United States, the world's strongest power, held the reins with inexperienced hands, while the Soviet Union moved like a massive glacier nearer the heart of Europe.

All of these depressing truths—and more—must have been foremost in the thoughts of those British leaders as the war moved closer to ultimate victory over the Germans in 1944. The kinds of questions and doubts that plagued their minds when thinking of the immediate future can only be guessed at; however, one British defense expert, C.J. Bartlett suggested that the most important questions in 1944-45 for the "little British donkey" were: "Of what value in such circumstances would be the world's second largest navy? Of what value in this new world of Asiatic nationalists would be Britain's traditional eastern strategic reserve—the Indian army? . . . How could Britain adopt her traditional policy of partial aloofness from the Continent and reliance on the balance of power when Russia might soon prove to be the only real power in Europe? Should Russia prove hostile, how could one blockade that virtually self-sufficient land mass? . . . Would even a second Battle of Britain prove feasible in the nuclear age? Could Bomber Command be developed into a viable instrument against so distant and huge a country, especially after its dependence on American assistance in its controversial contribution in the recent war?"[62]

Therefore, for Mr. Churchill and persons of like persuasion, the remaining months of the war in Europe were not just to be a time of anticipating the long-awaited victory. Indeed, what should have been a period of growing satisfaction and joy became instead a time of anxiety, frustration and increasing helplessness. There were desperate attempts to convince the United States of the increasing Soviet danger as Germany began to collapse completely and the mighty Russian army moved across Europe. Despite Roosevelt's midwar assumption that the Soviets would no doubt dominate the Baltic at war's end,[63] the British Prime Minister was not ready to accept it as fact.

As victory in Europe came nearer and the Soviet armies moved steadily westward, so British policy towards Germany came increasingly to be dominated by anxieties about the changing balance of power in Europe which this portended.[64] In other words, was there still a possibility of utilizing the deteriorating German situation to halt the Russians? The important element was, of course, the remaining German armed forces. Could a policy be employed that would deliberately place the bulk of surrendered German forces and arms in Western hands? Was Churchill seriously considering taking in the enemy forces as a junior partner if the United States did not back his stand against the Russians?

NOTES

1. R. A. Winnacker, "Yalta—another Munich?" in Robert Divine, ed., *Causes and Consequences of World War II* (Chicago: Quadrangle, 1969), p. 248.

2. "Our worst blunder of the War: Europe and the Russians," Ibid., pp. 167-68.

3. J. L. Gaddis, *The United States and the Origins of the Cold War, 1941-1948* (New York: Columbia University Press, 1972), p. 88.

4. "Strike from the South," in S. Bialer, ed., *Stalin and His Generals: Soviet Military Memoirs of World War II* (New York: Pegasus, 1969), p. 521.

5. *Memoirs of Dr. Eduard Beneš* (Boston: Houghton Mifflin, 1953), p. 240.

6. Ibid., p. 243 ff.

7. U. von Hassell, *The Von Hassell Diaries, 1938-1944* (New York: Doubleday, 1947), p. 327.

8. *Foreign Relations of the United States, 1943*, Vol. III (Washington, D.C.: U.S. Government Printing Office, 1963), pp. 623 and 690. Hereafter cited as *F.R.U.S.*

9. *Nazi Conspiracy and Aggression*, Supplement B (Washington, D.C.: U.S. Government Printing Office, 1946), pp. 1193-1204.

10. F. W. Deakin, *The Brutal Friendship* (New York: Anchor, 1966), pp. 264-65; and R. M. K. Kempner, "Stalin's 'Separate Peace' in 1943," *United Nations World*, 4 (March 1950), p. 7. The conference was held at Castle Klessheim near Salzburg in early April.

11. *History of the Second World War* (New York: G. P. Putnam, 1971), p. 488. The matter of a separate peace remains an intriguing theme for historians.

12. *Zwischen Hitler und Stalin, 1939-1945* (Bonn: Athenaeum, 1950), pp. 243 ff.

13. Ibid., pp. 246 ff.

14. Ibid., pp. 266, 267 and 274-275.

15. U.S. Records of the Joint Chiefs of Staff, CCS 334 Combined Chiefs of Staff (8-17-43), 113th Meeting, "Military considerations in relation to Russia," RG 218, pp. 5-6.

16. See A. Dallin, "Vlasov and separate peace: a note," *Journal of Central European History*, XVI (January 1957), pp. 394-96.

17. "Unconditional surrender," *The Contemporary Review*, Vol. 176 (October 1949), p. 193.

18. "The famous phrase 'unconditional surrender' was originally used by Grant on February 16, 1862; what he wanted was the surrender of Ft. Donelson by Confederate General Simon Bolivar Buckner . . . and that was what he got." H. Stein, ed., *American Civil-Military Decisions* (Birmingham, Alabama: University of Alabama Press, 1963), p. 308.

19. Cited in B. R. von Oppen, *Documents on Germany under Occupation, 1945-1954* (New York: Oxford University Press, 1955), p. 1. Much later, Churchill remarked that while he had indeed supported Roosevelt's unconditional surrender stand, it had not been the kind of statement that "we or our Government would have used." Ibid., p. 409. See also, E. Roosevelt, *As He Saw It* (New York: Duell, Sloan and Pearce, 1946), p. 117.

20. *The Hinge of Fate* (Boston: Houghton Mifflin, 1950), pp. 684-86.

21. G. Ritter, *The German Resistance* (New York: Praeger, 1958), p. 273.

22. E. Krantkraemer, *Deutsche Geschichte nach dem zweiten Weltkrieg* (Hildesheim: August Lax, 1962), pp. 11-12.

23. J. P. Warburg, *Germany–Bridge or Battleground?* (London: Heinemann, 1947), p. 260.

24. Loc. cit.

25. See *F.R.U.S., 1945*, Vol. III, p. 719; and D. Lerner, *Sykewar: Psychological Warfare against Germany, D-Day to VE-Day* (New York: George W. Stewart, 1949), p. 134.

26. U.S. National Archives, Foreign Military Studies Monographs, Series Number MS #P-202, German copy, "The significance to the Germans during World War II of the Allied term 'Unconditional Surrender,' " n.d., pp. 23-24.

27. J. L. Chase, "Unconditional Surrender reconsidered," *Political Science Quarterly*, LXX, No. 2 (June 1955), p. 271.

28. See A. Bryant, *The Turn of the Tide, 1939-1943* (London: Collins, 1957); and S. E. Morison, *Strategy and Compromise* (Boston: Little, Brown, 1958).

29. A. Werth, *The Year of Stalingrad* (New York: Alfred A. Knopf, 1947).

30. T. Higgins, *Winston Churchill and the Second Front, 1940-1943* (London: Oxford University Press, 1947), pp. 71-74.

31. J. M. Burns, *Roosevelt: The Soldier of Freedom* (New York: Harcourt Brace Jovanovich, 1970), p. 233.

32. H. H. Adams, *1942: The Year that Doomed the Axis* (New York: David McKay 1967), p. 229.

33. Burns, op. cit., p. 237.

34. F. C. Pogue, *George C. Marshall: Organizer of Victory, 1943-1945* (New York: Viking, 1973), p. 237.

35. Werth, op. cit., pp. 263-64.

36. Ibid., pp. 272-73.

37. F. Morgan, *Overture to Overlord* (New York: Doubleday, 1950), p. 26.

38. G. Harrison, *Cross-Channel Attack* (Washington, D.C.: U.S. Government Printing Office, 1951), pp. 79-81.

39. Morgan, op. cit., p. 106.

40. Ibid., pp. 107-114.

41. *F.R.U.S., The Conference at Washington and Quebec, 1943* (Washington, D.C.: 1970), pp. 910-11. Pogue made note of the General's concern at Quebec in writing that, "For only a moment the curtain was raised on a question that was later to loom large in Western thinking. But the point was not explored." Op. cit., p. 249.

42. *F.R.U.S., The Conference at Washington and Quebec, 1943*, pp. 910-11.

43. F. Williams, *A Prime Minister Remembers* (London: Heinemann, 1961), p. 76.

44. *F.R.U.S., The Conference at Washington and Quebec, 1943*, p. 76; and Beneš, *Memoirs*, p. 187.

45. Beneš's personal secretary accompanied the Czech leader on his U.S. trip and later wrote that Beneš had already begun his memoirs and did *not* include all he could have for political reasons. E. Tabersky, "Beneš and Stalin–Moscow, 1943 and 1945," *Journal of Central European Affairs*, XIII (July 1953), p. 155.

46. Beneš, *Memoirs*, p. 342.

47. Loc. cit.

48. Morgan, *Overture to Overlord*, p. 122.

49. O. Bradley, *A Soldier's Story* (New York: Henry Holt, 1951), p. 199.

50. M. Matloff, "The Soviet Union and the War in the West," in A. Eisenstadt, ed., *American History: Recent Interpretations* (New York: Thomas Y. Crowell, 1962), p. 424.

51. Burns, *Roosevelt*, p. 238.

52. *F.R.U.S., The Conferences at Cairo and Teheran* (Washington, D.C.: 1961), p. 553.

53. Loc. cit.

54. Ibid., pp. 583-84.

55. Loc. cit.

56. "Baroness Asquith of Yarnbury in conversation with Kenneth Harris," *The Listener*, August 17, 1967, p. 199. See also A. Harriman and E. Abel, *Special Envoy to Churchill and Stalin, 1941-1946* (New York: Random House, 1975), p. 170.

57. J. Wheeler-Bennett and A. Nichols, *The Semblance of Peace* (New York: St. Martin's, 1972), p. 290.

58. A. Bryant, *Triumph in the West* (New York: Doubleday, 1949), p. 49.

59. E. Roosevelt, *As He Saw It*, pp. 184-85.

60. Baldwin, "Our worst blunder in the War," in Divine, *Causes and Consequences*, p. 172.

61. J. Leasor, *War at the Top* (London: Michael Joseph, 1959), pp. 13 and 283. For a similar view, see W. Strang, *Britain in World Affairs* (New York: Praeger, 1961), pp. 337-38. In light of the British criticism over the lack of political concern shown by U.S. military leaders, the following account given by Eisenhower is somewhat ironic. He related that one time during the war the bombing of Italy was halted for about a week because of an equipment shortage. He decided to use the time to tell the Italians that now was the opportune moment to surrender; however, it soon came back to him that Churchill had immediately complained to F.D.R. that soldiers were supposed to fight and leave politics to the politicians. J. Nelson, ed., *A Conversation with Alistair Cooke: General Eisenhower on the Military Churchill* (New York: W.W. Norton, 1970), pp. 54-55.

62. C. J. Bartlett, *The Long Retreat: A Short History of British Defense Policy, 1945-1970* (London: Macmillan, 1972), p. 8.

63. See Gaddis, *U.S. and Origins of Cold War,* p. 135.

64. D. C. Watt, *Britain Looks to Germany: British Opinion and Policy towards Germany since 1945* (London: Oswald Wolff, 1965), pp. 44-45.

Chapter 3

TROUBLED VICTORY

There was little doubt that 1945 would witness the total collapse of Hitler's empire, and Allied forces renewed their efforts toward that end. It may be wrong to assume that in all quarters this implied utilizing the most rapid means of beating the German armies. Was it possible that to Churchill, "the quick defeat of Germany be damned, the British Empire wanted British troops in Berlin before the Russians got there and, en route, wanted British troops in Hamburg and Bremen, which it was feared the Russians might occupy and try to hold at the conference table?"[1]

Relations between Great Britain and the United States were no longer dominated by a common enemy to be beaten at all cost, and although the winter of 1944-45 had seen temporary delays in invading the German homeland, her destiny had really been sealed with the successful Normandy landing. Therefore, with the "anvil of necessity" out of the way, it was time to turn to other important considerations. "To Churchill, warily watching the swift Soviet advance into Poland and the Balkans, the war had become more than ever a contest for great political stakes, and he wished Western Allied strength diverted to forestall the Russian surge."[2]

The possibility of a Western confrontation with the advancing Soviets was not lost upon the Nazi leadership. Hitler had already been informed in January 1945 of Allied plans for dealing with a defeated Germany, and any evidence of a rift between the West and Russia was good news indeed. General Walter Warlimont, present at Hitler's headquarters during this period, wrote that it was the Fuehrer's "conviction that the enemy coalition would collapse, and he was continually thinking that he had discovered new indications of it."[3]

Despite the growing concerns, although for very different reasons, of Churchill and Hitler, the Yalta meeting in February reaffirmed Roosevelt's desire to lay further groundwork for post-war planning together with the Soviets. Basic work had already been completed specifying terms on the demilitarization of Germany, indicating clearly that the defeated forces were to be immediately disbanded and arms destroyed: "No German military organization by whatever name or designation, or in whatever form or guise, is permitted to be established or operate in Germany or abroad."[4]

Meanwhile, however, the Allied breach was widening on the question of interpreting Russian intentions, and even the close relationship Churchill had enjoyed with Roosevelt was disappearing. "I was no longer being fully heard by him," wrote the British Prime Minister in the days just after Yalta, "I did not know how ill he was, or I might have felt it cruel to press him."[5]

The British leader had already expressed his opposition to the plan for the dismembering of Germany,[6] "until my doubts about Russia's intentions have been cleared away."[7] Although the British Foreign Office was critical of the Prime Minister's stand, he did have the Chief of Staff on his side, and a decidedly more militant stance toward the Russians was soon evident. Churchill was also supported by his cabinet, for their attitude too indicated a readiness "to use military forces for clear political purposes. . . . It was not a point of view which was popular in the United States at that time."[8]

By March 1945, the collapse of the German armies was imminent, and news on the home front was equally horrifying with accounts of Soviet rape and plunder as they moved westward.[9] German newspapers, while warning against the spread of rumor, were already circulating daily dispatches reporting serious rifts

between Russia and the West.[10] In a desperate attempt to influence the advancing American and British soldiers, the Germans
deluged them with propaganda leaflets warning of a Red victory
and the demise of democracy. "To the Anglo-American it would
mean the swelling of the Russian Army to more than two hundred
divisions all of which would be employed against the Allied Front
to gain the supremccy [sic] of BOLSHEVISM."[11]

Meanwhile, renewed attempts during February-March at effect-
ing a peace in the West occupied a variety of personages on both
sides. Earlier, in January a high-ranking German SS officer sta-
tioned in northern Italy had begun to explore the possibilities of a
complete surrender of forces in that theater to the Western Allies.
Contact was made and a bit of the groundwork was prepared for
further discussion. One of the German participants later wrote
that in these preliminary talks, the Allies were continually assured
that "we did not intend for our peace attempts to drive a wedge
between the allies," but confided that the very statement "worked
wonders."[12]

By the tenth of March, the American President was informed
that German SS General Wolff, apparently with the tentative
approval of the Commander in Chief West, Field Marshal Albert
Kesselring, was in Switzerland ready to discuss details for surrendering the German forces.[13] As the "Bern affair" progressed—
the British and American legations in the Swiss capital had been
designated as the meeting places—the Soviet government was
informed and invited to send representatives. No immediate objec
tions were forthcoming and the Foreign Minister Molotov agreed
that such talks could prove important and indicated interest in
participation. Since observation and participation obviously meant
two different things, the Western Allies were hesitant to acquiesce
in a matter they regarded as a predominantly Western negotiation,
at least for the moment.

The entire question of a German surrender through Wolff and
Kesselring was a purely military affair in the first stages of discussion. To turn the Russian request down flat meant the possibility of starting a "surrender race," but since speed was deemed
necessary and Russian representatives, having no diplomatic
mission in Switzerland, could be indefinitely delayed, the Allied
decision was to push ahead and patch up any wounded feelings
later.[14]

Actually, the decision concerning any matter to be discussed at Bern was made at the Caserta headquarters of the Allied Commander for the Mediterranean, Field Marshal Alexander. "The British Chiefs of Staff consider Field Marshal Alexander . . . should alone be responsible for conducting the negotiations and reaching decisions. The position of the Russians will thus be virtually that of 'observers.' "[15] Although the British Foreign Office cautioned against placing the Russians strictly in the "observer" category in fear of like treatment on the eastern front, U.S. Ambassador to Russia, Harriman, advised a tough stand for he detected an increasing Soviet arrogance toward the Western Allies.[16]

By March 20, a rather firm U.S.-British position had emerged toward the pursuit of the Bern talks despite Soviet objections.[17] In fact, a reply was drafted to Russia over the signature of the British Ambassador in Moscow which indicated quite definitely the Allied determination to proceed while at the same time clearly defining the Soviet position as that of an invited observer. Reaction was fast and strong as Molotov charged in no uncertain terms that the British and Americans were engaging in negotiations with the enemy "behind the back of the Soviet government, which has been carrying on the main burden of the war against Germany."[18]

This was tough language indeed and brought a quick reply from the highest level. President Roosevelt drafted the answer directly to Stalin, and rejecting Molotov's charges out of hand, told the Soviet dictator that the negotiations violated nothing "of our agreed principle of unconditional surrender" and would, therefore, continue as long as fruitful. Stalin wrote that he agreed that the aim of war was to get the enemy to surrender, but he defended Molotov's words and insisted that the Bern talks were not speeding the war's end. He openly implied that Roosevelt was not fully informed, for the Germans were only stalling for time in order to move their troops from Italy to the eastern front, and, in fact, had already transferred three divisions. Thus, the Molotov request for direct participation in the Bern affair was for a very good reason. The Soviet leader stated that a violation of agreement was taking place.[19]

By month's end, Roosevelt was forced to admit that the entire episode had resulted in bringing "an atmosphere of regrettable apprehension and mistrust." He denied that discussions at Bern had allowed German troop movements from northern Italy to the Russian front and labeled Stalin's statement an "error." The American President insisted that no negotiations had actually taken place, but Stalin refused to be persuaded, and hewing to his original premise that the Allies were denying proper Soviet representation, he wrote:

> It may be assumed that you have not been fully informed. As regards my military colleagues, they, on the basis of data which they have on hand, do not have any doubts, that the negotiations have taken place and that they have ended in an agreement with the Germans, on the basis of which the German commander on the Western front Marshal Kesselring—has agreed to open the front and permit the Anglo-American troops to advance to the East, and the Anglo-Americans have promised in return to ease for the Germans the peace terms. . . .
>
> *I also cannot understand the silence of the British who have allowed you to correspond with me on this unpleasant matter, and they themselves remain silent, although it is known that the initiative in this whole affair with the negotiations in Bern belongs to the British.*[20]

It was now early April, and in light of the stand taken by Stalin toward the Bern affair, the British government proposed that the Western Allies adopt a clear policy on possible German approaches to surrender. For example, if the Germans offered total surrender, then the acceptance would have to be governed by existing agreement (Secret Moscow Protocol of November 1, 1943, i.e., the three governments were pledged "to concerting their actions"). However, a second alternative had begun to materialize which the British aide-memoire carefully described as "a purely military surrender on a single front." The British view was that in this second instance "it would be sufficient . . . if the Soviet government were kept informed through military channels of what is going on."[21]

Meanwhile, the Roosevelt-Stalin correspondence continued with the American leader reiterating his original stand that what was happening in Bern was exactly as had been described in earlier messages. He chided Stalin for his fears of partial surrender in the west and reminded him that he, Roosevelt, had specifically instructed General Eisenhower to accept unconditional terms only.[22]

Two points should be noted in regard to these events. One, the policy ordered by Churchill and executed by Alexander and later Montgomery, was certainly in opposition to the spirit of Roosevelt's exchange with Stalin. Secondly, it is also apparent that the American President continued to act in a manner that indicated either an unawareness of the growing Anglo-American breach or a decision to ignore it.

On April 5, Churchill assured F.D.R. of the fullest support in rebutting Stalin and characterized the messages from the Soviet dictator as insulting. This came from Soviet frustration, he wrote, and the fact that the Western Allies were on the verge of a victory while the Russians were still preparing for the next attack in mid-May. The Prime Minister suggested that there was more reason than ever now for the United States and Great Britain to push as far eastward as quickly as possible and even to take Berlin. "I believe," Churchill wrote, "this is the best chance of saving the future. If they are convinced that we are afraid of them and can be bullied into submission, then indeed I should despair of our future relations with them and much else."[23]

Several times in his communications to Roosevelt, Stalin defended his outrage on the basis of the intelligence information he was receiving and repeatedly emphasized the reliability of his sources. Insisting that the facts did not lie, Stalin pointed out that while the Germans were fighting to the death to hold worthless ground on the eastern front, they surrendered without resistance important cities in the west such as Osnabrueck, Mannheim and Kassel. "Don't you agree," he asked Roosevelt, "that such a behavior of the Germans is more than strange and incomprehensible?"[24] By this date, early April, the Bern talks were losing steam and all concerned were becoming impatient at the lack of progress, so the negotiations were broken off; on April 12, Roosevelt so notified the Soviet head.[25]

The matter did not rest there, however, for Wolff, before being recalled to Berlin, had written Himmler of the great importance of the Bern talks and pleaded with him to try and save Germany from total destruction. Impressed by Wolff's communiqué, Himmler contacted Count Folke Bernadotte, President of the Swedish Red Cross,[26] and told him that Hitler was finished, but that he, Himmler, had full authority to act and requested a meeting be arranged with Eisenhower. Himmler agreed to order the surrender of German forces all along the western front even including Denmark and Norway; he offered no surrender on the eastern front. Meanwhile, with Roosevelt's death, Churchill was in communication with President Truman about the probable offer and suggested that there be no acceptance of a surrender of the German government as such by Himmler unless on all fronts simultaneously, but carefully pointed out that the situation did not preclude "local surrenders as they occur."[27]

It was obvious that with the imminent collapse of Germany and the question of surrender not proceeding according to the unconditional formula, field commanders were beginning to play a more dominant role than the government heads in deciding exactly when and how the war would end. Despite this situation, Stalin requested his Western allies to prevent massive German retreats into their territory. "The Germans were fleeing from Rokossovsky [commander of the Second Belorussian Army] and surrendering to the English in a region occupied by Montgomery," Nikita Khrushchev later wrote, and "Stalin asked the English not to take prisoners and to compel the Germans to surrender to our troops. 'But nothing of the sort!' said Stalin angrily."[28]

As early as the first week of April, large numbers of German troops and civilians were fleeing westward. In large measure, however, Stalin had his own people to thank for that as well as the stiff resistance from those German troops that remained. As one writer phrased it, stopping "the Russians became a blind, desperate reflex action imposed by the terrifying image of Russian control."[29]

The evidence would indicate that Stalin was correct in his charge that the Germans were making a greater effort on the eastern front than they were in the west. Colonel General Rendulic, commander of the German Army Group South and charged with the defense of the Donau Valley and Vienna, wrote that about April 6, with the Russians in front and the Americans in the rear, he received the following Fuehrer directive: "It is decisive for the fate of the Reich that the Eastern Front be held. The Americans, however, are to be offered purely delaying resistance, for the sake of honor."[30] A similar evaluation came from the German forces in the northwest. General Gustave Hoehne, part of Field Marshal Busch's command, wrote that by April 10 there was already a general acceptance that the Anglo-American advance would be fast and "neither the [German] troops nor their leaders were determined any longer to delay [it]. . . . Everything was dominated by the *East.* Each day we or the staffs made a more thorough study of the situation in the *East* than that in the West immediately before us."[31]

A difficult—if not impossible—problem that confronted German commanders caught between the fronts with orders to allow the Western advance while delaying the Russians, was the question of supplies. One of the generals put it this way: "Should the Western enemy gain access to the supply area of the Army Group, it would be quite impossible to continue fighting on the Eastern Front."[32]

A unique propaganda opportunity was now presented to both the Western Allies and the Russians, for the war had brought the German troops literally within shouting distance of their enemies at various points on the battle fronts. One of America's psychological warriors described the moment thusly: "All [German] soldiers could hear the direct broadcasts addressed to them from our mobile loudspeakers, which sometimes operated within a few hundred yards of the enemy's most advanced positions."[33]

Of course, the usual entreaties to surrender could now be transmitted orally and, no doubt, with greater relevance and immediacy than ever before. A bizarre twist was added with the exploitation of current rumor that the collapsing German armies were soon going to join a Western crusade against Bolshevism. One such account by an American general describing the fighting near Magdeburg about April 13, read:

> then one POW gave us the info that the people fighting us were putting out the story that as the Russians came up, we would switch sides and join the Germans in fighting them. We figured they were maybe whistling to keep their courage up. But it was still an opening. So we put it out over the loudspeakers that the story was true. Whether they gave the G's what seemed to be an honorable way out, at least it almost at once collapsed resistance . . . and many of them came in with their hands up.[34]

British propagandists engaged in like activity with the loudspeakers from their lines in the northwest urging German soldiers to surrender since it would be much preferable to be "taken prisoner by the British since the Russians were approaching."[35]

The American General Walter Bedell Smith, later Ambassador to the Soviet Union, expressed amazement that the Russians really seemed to believe the possibility of a Western-German coalition of some kind emerging and noted that Russian loudspeakers too were busy advising the German troops that to surrender to the British and Americans meant being used soon in an offensive against the Soviet Union.[36] The Russian propagandists told the German soldiers that "the greatest betrayal in the history of mankind is in preparation. If you do not wish to continue fighting against us side by side with the forces of Capitalism, come over to us."[37]

Of course, a major concern now for Churchill was to halt the Russians as far east as possible, and he confided his growing fears to Anthony Eden, Secretary of State for Foreign Affairs. On April 18, Eden told the Prime Minister that he fully shared these anxieties and supported the view that Montgomery should move into Luebeck as quickly as possible. "A Russian occupation of Denmark," Eden wrote, "would cause us much embarrassment."[38] Churchill, already lamenting the loss of Berlin to the Russians, felt that although there was no good reason for them to take Denmark, "our position at Luebeck, if we get it, would be decisive in this matter."[39]

Interestingly, Montgomery felt the need for additional forces for this task and requested an American army corps. The American General Omar Bradley described the British request, which was granted, as follows: "When Zhukov mounted his Berlin offensive, the British became more vehement in their plea. For unless Monty soon gained the Baltic, they argued, we would awaken to find the Red Army in Denmark and the Soviets on the North Sea."[40] Montgomery insisted that both Churchill and Eisenhower had sent him messages about the danger, urging him to "head off" the Russians before they got into Schleswig-Holstein and Denmark. He concluded that in so "far as I was concerned, the oncoming Russians were more dangerous than the stricken Germans."[41]

On Tuesday, May 1, 1945, the German radio began broadcasting the news of Hitler's death. It was stated that the Fuehrer had fallen in defense of Germany and had drawn his final breath fighting Bolshevism. Admiral Karl Doenitz was named his successor and immediately informed the German people that Hitler's life had been one of complete dedication to fighting communism and promised to protect them from being annihilated by the advancing Soviet armies.[42] (Of course, Hitler had not died fighting the Russians, or anybody else for that matter, but had taken poison on April 30, 1945.)[43]

The same day that Doenitz assumed control of government, he issued an order to the military forces that the "fight against the Americans and the English will continue as long as they hinder the battle against Bolshevism."[44] Obviously, such a command had little real meaning in light of the fact that the war was to end within the next few days; however, there was a certain significance in continuing the war cry against Russia, for it bolstered the rapidly spreading belief among many Germans that a reversal was still possible. Their desperate hopes rested entirely on the expectation of a break between the Western Allies and Russia, and a continuance of the war on the eastern front as a result.

This belief in the remote possibility of "a reversal of alliance" was one of the major reasons that Doenitz did not arrange for immediate surrender.[45] If the Grand Admiral had been able to read Montgomery's mind at that particular moment, he probably would have been convinced of an Allied-Russian break, for the British leader wrote, "I knew the German war was practically over. The essential and immediate task was to push on with all speed and get to the Baltic, and then form a flank facing east."[46] Marshal Konstantin Rokossovsky faced Montgomery across the "flank" and was quick to protest the British action, noting that their troops had deliberately landed behind the Russian front in an attempt to claim greater territory.[47]

On the German side it appeared that at all levels there was a strong feeling of an East-West conflict materializing. Propaganda Minister Goebbels had already broadcast the beginnings of just such a struggle in the contest for Berlin. A German colleague of the Minister who remained in the Berlin bunker during those last frantic days, wrote that Goebbels "had actually got the majority of German soldiers who are defending Berlin, believing his whispering campaign that at any moment the Americans are coming to their aid against the Russians."[48] A diary entry of a German soldier reflected the near hysteria that swept the ranks as rumor upon rumor spread; he wrote that everyone thought that the Americans would soon free all the German prisoners, arm them, and march against the Bolsheviks. The idea seemed to evoke wild

enthusiasm, for he observed that everybody "wants to continue . . . against the Russians; it doesn't matter how long the war
lasts!"[49] A German army captain told that his commanding general had personally informed him that everything was being
arranged in order that the war in the east would continue now
with British aid.[50]

According to Russian Marshal V.I. Chuikov, the Germans did
not want to overlook any possibility and therefore, General Krebs,
Chief of the German army general staff, approached him on May 1
with the request for an armistice. Chuikov said that Krebs was
really trying to "find out whether there was not something to be
gained by playing on our well-founded feelings of distrust toward
our allies."[51]

The crucial problem for Doenitz, however, was to continue to
maneuver his forces in a rapidly shrinking state in such a manner
as to prevent mass surrender or capture on the eastern front while
preventing at the same time a total collapse in the west. He was
generally well aware of the zones of occupation that the Allies
would assume upon war's end, and now the trick was to facilitate
a mass westward movement into American and British zones
before the final shot was fired. This meant a monumental task
involving the transfer of millions of Germans on a timetable that
had to be revised from hour to hour. The Grand Admiral confronted a frightening dilemma for he had to avoid a last-ditch
slaughter and at the same time delay as long as possible final
capitulation.

Quite obviously Doenitz's options were severely limited and
getting smaller by the minute, and his task of aiding many of his
countrymen to escape Russian captivity and domination was
accomplished in an atmosphere of the most extreme chaos and
desperation. A description by General Tippelskirsch catches the
mood: "The road[s] . . . were littered with abandoned vehicles
and weapons and crowded with fleeing soldiers—a picture which
was shocking, but at the same time reassuring; it showed that the
last final efforts to save an army from Russian prison camps were
working."[52]

From the time of his appointment until surrender became
unavoidable, Doenitz hoped to gain eight to ten days for his
mission of rescuing millions of Germans from the Russian grasp.
He later felt that his plan had been immensely successful, for just

after hostilities he "related how he had organized a radio campaign which induced an estimated million German [civilians] to flee westward to escape the Russians. He boasted that he had arranged to bring out the ablest Germans, particularly the scientists, who could be most useful to the West."[53]

Not only did Doenitz gain his eight to ten days, but he continued to move Germans westward even after the war had ended (see below)! An important point not acknowledged by western authorities was also the fact that the German Admiral had carried out a gradual surrender policy to the West instead of the unconditional terms demanded. The decisive element that allowed this was the willingness of Churchill and Montgomery to accept German military surrender of large numbers of troops in the final days of the war without demanding total surrender on all fronts as a precondition. The temptation to take into custody over two million German soldiers (with weapons) was too great. Coupled with the fears of Churchill and Montgomery about the Russian advance, this proved crucial in the British course of action.

In anticipating a situation without the support of the United States, the Prime Minister was ready to use any source available to him, while at the same time "he thought that the further east he was the better he would be able to fight Uncle Joe."[54] It was in this brief period of ending warfare that the dramatic decision to thwart the Russian advance at all costs was made by Winston Churchill. It was clearly a unilateral choice that could only be implemented by the most desperate of measures.

It had quickly become apparent to Doenitz that he had a more willing "collaborator" in the British than in the Americans for his scheme of gradual surrender. Any number of sources attest to the fact that before the final surrender on the seventh of May, Montgomery had gathered up numerous German forces and had allowed the westward movement of German civilians. Most of this occurred between the second and the sixth of May. One eyewitness to these events was the German General Gustave Hoehne who described the willingness of the British to allow passage west "as long as British troop movements would not be hampered. At the same time the military . . . surrender to the British . . . was completed . . . under conditions favorable to us. . . . All batteries were handed over to the British undamaged and just as they were. . . . The use of the phrase 'capitulation on the field of battle' was granted."[5] [5]

Admiral Doenitz's government had already begun to take some shape by May 2, for he had appointed a cabinet, taken up quarters in Flensburg, and started to assume the role of head of Germany's new regime. The conviction that the struggle against Russia would continue was expressed by his newly appointed foreign minister, Count Schwerin von Krosigk, in a radio address to the German people on that same day. In reference to the establishment of the United Nations in San Francisco, von Krosigk scoffed at the idea of world peace while Bolshevism was consuming Europe; reflecting Doenitz's theme he told his listeners that for four long years they had fought without parallel as a bulwark against "the Red flood. Germany could have protected Europe from Bolshevism if its rear had been freed."[5] [6]

The German determination to continue the fight against Russia never lost its strength even in the worst of moments, for on the very day of von Krosigk's broadcast, Kesselring notified the Grand Admiral that he felt there was still a possibility to pursue the war against the Bolsheviks with the remainder of Germany's armies.[5] [7]

Kesselring, now Commander in Chief of all German armies in the south, had already requested the Allies not to announce the surrender of forces in Italy in order to allow more time to move soldiers westward. Although Eisenhower did not feel that there was any reason to delay the news, he appeared completely unaware of Kesselring's motives or the dimensions of the German westward movement.[58]

On the evening of that same day, May 2, Doenitz had already commissioned a delegation headed by Admiral Hans von Friedeburg to visit Montgomery's headquarters. The British Marshal met Friedeburg, who now held Doenitz's old job as head of the German navy, and General Eberhardt Kinzel at noon the following day.[59] Montgomery described the meeting in these words:

> Admiral Friedeburg . . . read me a letter from Field Marshal Keitel offering to surrender to me the three German armies withdrawing in front of the Russians between Berlin and Rostock. I refused to consider this, saying that these armies should surrender to the Russians. I added that, of course, if any German soldiers came towards my front with their hands up, they would automatically be taken prisoners.[60]

Montgomery's last sentence contained the most important words for Doenitz because it meant that the western avenue of escape was still open. Montgomery's decision was definitely not in the spirit of "unconditional surrender," nor in accordance with Eisenhower's instructions. Some contemporary observers felt that with the surrender of Germany's Third Panzer Division and Twelfth and Twenty-first armies, Montgomery could not conceal his elation at gathering in over a million troops in one grand action. "I am dealing with the command of forces facing me," he said to those assembled for the meeting with Friedeburg, "and I have absolutely excluded anything that might be an Allied matter."[61] Again, one cannot ignore the careful reference to the German surrender as entirely Montgomery's business and responsibility at the given moment. Of course, Montgomery might have refused to accept formal surrender for he already had the bulk of German forces facing him in his hands.[62]

It is clear that those German leaders who dealt with Montgomery during the final week of war instantly recognized that he reflected a strong and distinct anti-Russian bias and they were quick to seize whatever advantage it offered. Von Friedeburg sensed that, despite his cool exterior, the British Field Marshal had clear reservations about the Russians.[63] When the details of Friedeburg's mission were known at Doenitz's headquarters in Flensburg—Montgomery had asked for the surrender of all German forces in Holland, the Friesen Islands, Schleswig-Holstein, Helgoland, and Denmark—the immediate reaction was that unconditional surrender had been avoided and that the continued transport of German troops and civilians westward could continue. The German assumption was also that Montgomery had agreed to refer the question of an extraterritorial enclave for Doenitz's government to higher headquarters.[64]

Doenitz quickly agreed to Montgoméry's demands for the additional territorial surrenders for the areas in question could no longer be controlled, and Eisenhower voiced no objection to this. From Doenitz's standpoint, however, there was no doubt that a partial surrender in the west had indeed been achieved. The old Admiral later wrote: "The discussion concerning a partial surrender took place on May 3, 1945 between Montgomery and von Friedeburg, whom I had sent to the British Fieldmarshal for this purpose."[65]

On that same day, Churchill received reports from Sweden that a small Russian scouting party had already parachuted into southeastern Zealand in Denmark while Soviet troops were arriving in force at Warnemuende with the clear implication of occupying Denmark. The Prime Minister, after some heated debate with his cabinet, notified Generals Eisenhower and Montgomery.[66] The truth of the matter, as clarified in an additional Swedish report, was that the Russian landing party in Zealand consisted of two men, while a few Soviet agents had accompanied the flow of German refugees into Denmark. The Russians did, however, later occupy the Danish island of Bornholm.[67]

Meanwhile, Montgomery moved ahead with all speed to complete the surrender along his front and bring the Russian advance to a rapid standstill. On May 4, Friedeburg handed over all control of German forces and territories agreed upon with Montgomery the previous day.[68] "Montgomery had decided to take just his due—which, after all, included the notable booty of Holland and Denmark and what was left of Germany—and then pass the negotiations on to S.H.A.E.F. for the final overall surrender," so wrote one British admirer.[69] Khrushchev had a somewhat different recollection of the incident as he remembered Stalin's angry outbursts, "Montgomery took them all, and he took their arms. So the fruits of our victory over the Germans were being enjoyed by Montgomery!"[70] At ths point Eisenhower ordered that there would be no further surrender until there was complete coordination with his headquarters. The order specifically included Norway.[71]

There was no question of the strategic value of Norway in Doenitz's mind, for there were nearly half a million Germans in that country who could be utilized. He had already dispatched some people to Stavanger in Northern Norway to prepare for just such a contingency.[72] Germany had long recognized Norway as a potential invasion point by the Allies and therefore maintained large forces there. Since Norway did not become a combat zone at war's end, the German troops there remained relatively fresh and ready for battle.[73]

Allied plans for occupying Norway had actually been long under consideration, and in the summer of 1944 there was general agreement that the country really belonged within the sphere of Western operations, even though there existed no specific agreement with the Russians on the matter. "Our purpose must be . . .

to avoid any clash with the Russians in Norway," so read a cable from the Combined Chiefs of Staff. "Nevertheless, if the Russians enter Norway during the course of operations against the Germans, it is considered undesirable for us to intervene."[74]

May 1945 was not September 1944. What was desirable at one time was not at another, and some of the Allies were very determined to include Norway in the western regional surrender. It was plain that Eisenhower had somewhat mixed feelings for he certainly did not intend for Montgomery to scoop it up in his grand slam in northwestern Europe. Not only was it ridiculing the whole unconditional surrender principle, but the Supreme Commander had already ordered that there be no additional surrenders accepted until he had agreed to them and he meant by this a total surrender on all fronts, the Russian included.[75]

Of course, considering Doenitz's self-appointed mission of rescuing Germans for the West, Norway represented the last pawn to be played in his stalling for time. On May 4 there was a Wehrmacht strength in Norway of some 340,000 men supported by about 27,000 German para-military and civilians. In addition, there were 87,000 prisoners of war—most of them Russian nationals.[76] Despite Eisenhower's position, Norway was not surrendered by Doenitz until almost four days later. Schwerin von Krosigk, now acting foreign minister in Doenitz's cabinet, said that no one on the German side felt that partial surrenders would have any effect on the final surrender and therefore there was nothing to lose by continuing to play the cards to the bitter end.[77]

Allied leadership was not oblivious to Doenitz's game and Montgomery had, in fact, already turned it to a British advantage, but it was also clear that there were aspects of the situation that were really beyond anyone's control. The recognition that the Germans were just stalling for time was tempered by the certainty that absolute collapse was imminent. Even in this mood, however, Allied impatience was apparent in the final days and hours and on the fifth of May, as the final surrender process began, Eisenhower was still not convinced that Doenitz had abandoned a last effort to secure some sort of Western standstill in order to create a split between the West and the Russians.[78] The Supreme Commander had expressed these misgivings at dinner that very evening, and ironically, just before the arrival of Admiral von Friedeburg with a request for additional clarification of the surrender terms. "He was told that nothing less than unconditional surrender was acceptable. The hopelessness of the German military situation was then pointed out to him and he was urged to consider whether he should not obtain authority to sign," Eisenhower telegraphed the Combined Chiefs; "he is now drafting a cable to Admiral Doenitz which we believe contains the suggestion that he should receive authorization to sign."[79]

At the time Eisenhower's message was dispatched—perhaps at the very same hour—a message was being sent to all German army commanders from Doenitz which read: "When we lay down our arms in northwest Germany, Denmark and Holland, then it means we have lost all reason to continue the fight against the Western powers. However, in the east, the fight will go on and it may be possible to rescue more German people from Bolshevism and slavery. Every officer's honor is now at stake!"[80]

This message, including the news of surrender negotiations, did not reach General Rendulic's Army Group South, and he later described the dilemma he found himself in:

> Detailed instructions for the continuation of the battle had not reached Army Group by the evening of 5 May '45, nor was any explanation to be had. . . . Army Group had already considered the possibility that, upon reaching our lines, the Americans and British might join us in a continuation of the struggle against the Russians. This theory had now become critical and the final moment to ascertain its validity had definitely arrived. Above and beyond the attitude and behavior of the Russians [who were broadcasting warnings against the West and urging the Germans to join them], there were other facts which made the idea seem probable. For example, numerous telephone lines and installations . . . were still intact, although they lay behind the American front lines. Furthermore, supply columns of the Army Group and of the American forces drew rations jointly from ration supply depots in upper Austria and drove along together on the same roads leading to the East.[81]

Rendulic further stated that the Russians were already preparing a defensive line against the West in the territory they had captured, "although not a single German bomber put in an appearance, the Russians immediately set the inhabitants of the villages . . . to work on the construction of air raid shelters and bunkers."[82]

To the north, Doenitz was still successfully prolonging the final negotiations and would continue to do so for another forty-eight hours. Around midnight of the fifth, American Undersecretary of State Robert Murphy notified the State Department that talks were expected to proceed through the night "as they[the Germans] apparently hoped to negotiate a surrender to SHAEF without the Russians; it is believed that after telegraphic consultation with Doenitz, they will sign probably tomorrow."[83]

Field Marshal Alfred Jodl arrived the next day and while the Allies assumed he carried full authorization to sign a final surrender, the German Marshal still contacted the Flensburg headquarters wih his assessment of the situation. He requested additional confirmation after concluding that "I don't see any other way out except chaos or sign."[84]

It was now clear that there was to be no formal surrender by a central German government and that the unconditional surrender instrument prepared by the European Advisory Commission would not serve. All the governments would have to proclaim the surrender on their own authority. "This course was the one adopted. Following upon the signature of the Acts of Military Surrender at Reims and Berlin on May 7 and 8 respectively, the Declaration was signed at Soviet Headquarters in Berlin on June 5, 1945."[85] While the Western Allies were completing the surrender at Reims, Stalin expressed strong doubts that the German forces on the eastern front would obey the cease-fire order. He informed President Truman that intercepted German radio messages pointed to plans for continued fighting, and therefore the Soviet leader had decided to wait until at least the ninth of May before announcing the news to his people that the Germans had been finally defeated.[86] The German people—at least those who listened or cared—were informed by radio on May 7 of the terms of surrender by Schwerin von Krosigk.

In a letter to his mother describing the surrender news, President Truman wrote that the British Prime Minister "began calling me at daylight to know if we shouldn't make an immediate release without considering the Russians. He was refused. . . . But he was mad as a wet hen."[87] In a story reported by Drew Middleton, detailing the surrender scene, the correspondent especially noted the British absence; "there is some comment here over the fact that Britain, the nation that first declared war on Germany, is not represented among the signatories."[88]

NOTES

1. R. Ingersoll, *Top Secret* (New York: Harcourt, Brace and Co., 1946), p. 324. An interesting note on this was a Churchill quote from January 11, 1945, in which the British P.M. urged caution in predicting war's end and suggested October 1945 as a safe possibility. *Triumph and Tragedy* (Boston: Houghton Mifflin, 1953), p. 731.

2. M. Matloff, "The Soviet Union and the War in the West," in A. Eisenstadt, ed., *American History: Recent Interpretations*, p. 428.

3. W. Warlimont, *Inside Hitler's Headquarters, 1939-1945* (New York: Praeger, 1964), p. 4.

4. *F.R.U.S., 1945*, Vol. III, pp. 424 ff.

5. Churchill, *Triumph and Tragedy*, p. 419.

6. *F.R.U.S., 1945*, Vol. III, pp. 430 ff.

7. C. Ryan, *The Last Battle* (New York: Simon and Schuster, 1966), p. 164.

8. M. P. Schoenfeld, *The War Ministry of Winston Churchill* (Ames, Iowa: Iowa State University Press, 1972), p. 242.

9. *Deutsche Allgemeine Zeitung*, February 23 and March 7, 1945.

10. See *Voelkischer Beobachter*, Munich ed., March 20, 22, 26 and 30, 1945.

11. Leaflet from the collection of Klaus Kirschner, Verlag fuer zeitgeschichtliche Dokumente und Curiosa, Erlangen, West Germany. Of course, Allied propaganda efforts were taking their toll on the western front by this date. See J. M. Erdmann, *Leaflet Operations in the Second World War* (Denver: Denver Instant Printing, 1969); and E. A. Shils and M. Janowitz, "Cohesion and disintegration in the Wehrmacht in World War II," *Public Opinion Quarterly*, Summer 1948, pp. 280-315.

12. R. Rahn, *Ruheloses Leben* (Duesseldorf: Diederichs, 1949), p. 282.

13. *F.R.U.S., 1945*, Vol. III, p. 722.

14. Ibid., pp. 724-27.

15. Ibid., p. 730.

16. Ibid., pp. 731-34.

17. On the 19th S.A.C. representatives had met Wolff in Bern and it was agreed that he would convey the discussions to Kesselring with an eye toward a full German surrender to the Allied headquarters at Caserta.

18. *F.R.U.S., 1945*, Vol. III, pp. 735-37.

19. Ibid., pp. 738-40. In an article called "Cold War origins 1," Paul Seabury wrote: "The logic of this new theory [that is, unconditional surrender on all fronts] would lead to the bleak notion that slaughter should have persisted on all fronts unless preliminary diplomatic contacts with the enemy in all cases would involve on-the-spot participation by all principal allies, who otherwise would become suspicious of each other." *The Journal of Contemporary History*, Vol. 3, No. 1 (January 1968), p. 114, fn. 5.

20. *F.R.U.S., 1945*, Vol. III, p. 742. Author's italics.

21. Ibid., p. 742. Interestingly, the U.S. response pointed out the inadvisability of presenting such suggestions at that time.

22. Ibid., pp. 745-46.

23. Ibid., pp. 746-47.

24. Ibid., p. 750. Writing after the war with the availability of German records, Seweryn Bailer noted that in the period April 11 to 20, 1945, German soldiers killed in the west numbered 577, with some 1,951 wounded; for the east, the figures were 7,587 German soldiers killed and 35,414 wounded. Bailer also wrote that for the same period, 268,229 Germans were "missing" on the west front, illustrating the large surrender figure there, as compared to only 25,823 Germans in the east. *Stalin and His Generals,* p. 621.

25. *F.R.U.S., 1945,* Vol. III, p. 750. For a German account, see R. Rahn, *Ruheloses Leben,* pp. 282 ff.

26. Rahn, *Ruheloses Leben,* p. 288.

27. *F.R.U.S., 1945,* Vol. III, pp. 759-62.

28. N. Khrushchev, *Khrushchev Remembers* (Boston: Little, Brown, 1970), pp. 221-22. Marshal Konstantin Rokossovsky was commanding officer of the Second Belorussian Army.

29. P. Kecskemeti, *Strategic Surrender* (Stanford: Stanford University Press, 1958), p. 153.

30. U.S. National Archives, Foreign Military Studies Monographs, Series Number MS #B-328, p. 4.

31. Ibid., MS #B-361, p. 5.

32. Ibid., MS #B-328, p. 9. The source of General Smith's information below may well have been this report by the German General Rendulic (n. 30 above), for it was called to his attention in 1947, by General Clarence Huebner, then United States Deputy Commander in Europe.

33. D. Lerner, *Sykewar,* p. 133.

34. Letter from General S.L.A. Marshall to author, August 30, 1971.

35. U.S. National Archives, Foreign Military Studies Monographs, Series Number MS #B-361, p. 11.

36. W. B. Smith, *Eisenhower's Six Great Decisions* (New York: Longmans, 1956), p. 224.

37. U.S. National Archives, Foreign Military Studies Monographs, Series Number MS #B-328, p. 4.

38. A. Eden, *The Memoirs of Anthony Eden: The Reckoning* (Boston: Houghton Mifflin, 1965), p. 612.

39. W. Churchill, *Triumph and Tragedy,* p. 515.

40. O. Bradley, *A Soldier's Story,* p. 546. Bradley wrote that since Patton's thrust down the Danube had dispelled all worry about a German redoubt, General Ridgeway's XVIII Airborne Corps was sent to Montgomery's aid.

41. B. L. Montgomery, *The Memoirs of Field Marshal, The Viscount Montgomery* (New York: World Publishing Co., 1958), p. 305. Later, Churchill insisted that Montgomery's action saved Luebeck with only hours to spare. *Triumph and Tragedy,* p. 539.

42. German Records Microfilmed at Alexandria, Va., Series 18, Reel 859, Frame 5605348-49, T-77.

43. L. Bezymenski, *The Death of Adolf Hitler* (New York: Harcourt, Brace and World, 1968), p. 75.

44. German Records Microfilmed at Alexandria, Va., 18/859/5605372, T-77.

45. See M. Steinert, *23 Days: The Final Collapse of Nazi Germany* (New York: Walker, 1969), pp. 174-75.

46. Montgomery, *Memoirs,* p. 299.

47. C. Whiting, *The End of the War, Europe, April 15-May 23, 1945* (New York: Stein and Day, 1973), p. 49.

48. G. Boldt, *Die Letzen Tage der Reichskanzlei* (Stuttgart: Rowohlt, 1947), p. 49.

49. K. Granzow, *Tagebuch eines Hitlerjungen, 1943-1945* (Bremen: C. Schoenemann, 1965), p. 177.

50. See D. Flower and J. Reeves, eds., *The Taste of Courage: Victory and Defeat* (New York: Berkley Medallion Ed., 1971), pp. 357-58; and J. Mueller, *Sturz in den Abgrund* (Offenbach am Main: Bollwerk, 1947), p. 77.

51. In Bailer, *Stalin and His Generals*, p. 536.

52. Quellen der Institut fuer Zeitgeschichte, Munich, unpublished manuscript Archive No. 160, Kurt von Tippelskirsch, Akz. Nr. 785/52, 00037.

53. R. Murphy, *Diplomat Among Warriors* (New York: Pyramid, 1965), pp. 272-73.

54. Whiting, *End of the War*, p. 26.

55. U.S. National Archives, Foreign Military Studies Monographs, MS #B-361, pp. 13-15.

56. German Records, 18/859/5605354/T-77.

57. Ibid., 5605049.

58. A. D. Chandler and S. E. Ambrose, eds., *The Papers of Dwight D. Eisenhower: The War Years* (Baltimore: Johns Hopkins, 1969), p. 2668.

59. C. Bekker, *Kampf und Untergang der Kriegsmarine* (Hannover: Adolf Sponholtz, 1953), p. 234.

60. Montgomery, *Memoirs*, p. 306.

61. R. W. Thompson, *Montgomery, The Field Marshal* (New York: Schribner's, 1969), p. 310.

62. Quellen der Institut fuer Zeitgeschichte, ms. Arch. No. 160, von Tippelskirsch, 785/52, 00037.

63. J. Thorwald, *Das Ende an der Elbe* (Stuttgart: Steingrueben, 1953), p. 197.

64. German Records, 18/867/5614038-41/T-77.

65. Letter to author, November 27, 1971.

66. British War Cabinet Minutes, War Cabinet 58(45), 4 May 1945, p. 336.

67. L. F. Ellis and A. E. Warhurst, *Victory in the West* (London: United Kingdom Series, 1968), p. 341.

68. M. Schulman, *Defeat in the West* (Westport, Conn.: Greenwood, 1948), p. 308. He added: "Another bit of the Wehrmacht to surrender before the official end was Army Group "G" under General Schultz, whose First and Nineteenth Armies laid down their arms in the Austrian Alps." Ibid., p. 309.

69. A. Moorhead, *Eclipse* (New York: Harper and Row, 1968), p. 284.

70. *Khrushchev Remembers*, p. 222.

71. *Eisenhower Papers: The War Years*, p. 2671.

72. Quellen der Institut fuer Zeitgeschichte, Arch. No. 1740, Eberhard Godt, 3190/63, 3-5.

73. E. F. Ziemke, *The German Northern Theater of Operations, 1940-1945* (Washington, D.C.: Dept. of Army Pamphlet 20-271, n.d.), p. 312.

74. *F.R.U.S., The Conference at Quebec, 1944*, pp. 400-01.

75. *Eisenhower Papers: The War Years*, p. 2671. In January 1945, British General Andrew Thorne had been appointed S.H.A.E.F. Mission Head for Norway.

76. Letter to author from the Historical Dept., Norwegian Armed Forces, April 4, 1972. One source placed the figure of Russian PW's at 83,000. H. L. Coles and A. K. Weinberg, *Civil Affairs: Soldiers Become Governors* (Washington, D.C.: U.S. Government Printing Office, 1964), p. 843.

77. *Christ und Welt*, Nr. 16, VIII Jahrgang (April 21, 1955).

78. H. C. Butcher, *My Three Years with Eisenhower* (New York: Simon and Schuster, 1946), p. 827.

79. *Eisenhower Papers: The War Years,* p. 2689.

80. German Records, 18/858/5604618/T077.

81. U.S. National Archives, Foreign Military Studies Monographs, MS #B-328, pp. 7-10.

82. Loc. cit.

83. *F.R.U.S., 1945,* Vol. III, p. 777.

84. German Records, 18/858/5004853/T-77.

85. W. Strang, *Home and Abroad* (London: Andre Deutsch, 1956), pp. 221-23. For a description of the surrender—a "comedy of errors"—see F. Pogue, *Supreme Command* (Washington, D.C.: U.S. Government Printing Office, 1954), pp. 484-85.

86. *F.R.U.S., 1945,* Vol. III, p. 779. In his study of the year 1945, B. Gardner wrote, "Stalin was not convinced that fighting would actually stop on the Eastern Front—and his doubt was well-founded." *The Year that Changed the World,* 1945 (New York: Coward-McCann, 1964), p. 149.

87. Harry S. Truman, *Memoirs,* Vol. I (New York: Signet, 1965), p. 232.

88. New York *Times,* May 9, 1945.

Chapter 4

GERMANY IN THE INITIAL POSTDEFEAT PERIOD

In the immediate days and weeks following the German surrender in May 1945, a very peculiar atmosphere prevailed. The joy of victory mingled with growing apprehensions about Soviet behavior presented disturbing contradictions. Obviously, most people remained unaware of the extent of Churchill's militant stance toward Russia. The critical events from April to May, when the Prime Minister's fears mounted daily and his growing hostility was expressed to leaders around him, were hidden from public view. There is no doubt that Churchill's determined attitude, supported by his readiness to translate it into action if need be, had some impact upon the American leaders as well, despite the confusions of war and the death of President Roosevelt. To describe the impact as one that modified policy toward a defeated Germany is not an exaggeration. Perhaps, to call the change a "policy" is too far-reaching, but to discern a clear and definite deviation from mutual wartime understanding is not. There was no exact time or act, however, that suddenly signaled a new awareness that wartime cooperation and agreement on dealing with a defeated German nation no longer existed.

Only in April had the draft of a directive on the "treatment of Germany in the Initial Post-Defeat period" been distributed to the

European Advisory Commission. Among other things, the directive specifically called for the complete and permanent disarmament of Germany and this included all para-military groups. In fact, this very directive was reviewed by the E.A.C. only four days before the official German surrender.[1]

The reality of the situation was different, however, and while an alternative policy could obviously not be offered since none had been developed, this only emphasized the fact that the entire situation was completely unexpected. There had been no "serious attempt to develop . . . plans for Germany in the light of possible difficulties with the Soviet Union."[2]

Of course, the incontrovertible truth was the continuance of some sort of German government at Flensburg with momentary Western acquiescence. The very presence of Grand Admiral Doenitz, Hitler's personally chosen successor, was proof of the changed Allied mood and indecision in the face of Soviet threat, real or imagined. In addition, it proved Churchill's strong determination to maintain any vestige of potential German support, Nazi or otherwise, against the Soviet Union.

It can only be concluded that the Doenitz regime continued to function until May 23 because Churchill wanted to preserve it. In the early May days of the 4th, 5th and 6th, Doenitz's entire structure was at the mercy of Field Marshal Montgomery, whose command now embraced Schleswig-Holstein and the Admiral's headquarters at Flensburg.

Later, much later, the following questions were asked of Churchill: "(1) on what authority General Montgomery refrained from arresting Grand Admiral Doenitz; . . . (2) on what authority General Montgomery permitted . . . Doenitz, between 4th and 23rd May, 1945, to form and operate . . . a government; . . . (3) on what authority General Montgomery permitted . . . Doenitz . . . to operate a broadcasting station at Flensburg; . . . and whether the broadcasts, including those in which the German troops and civilians were urged to cooperate . . . with a view to regaining lands they had lost to the Union of Soviet Socialist Republics, were authorized . . . by the British?"[3] These were questions put to Winston Churchill in 1954 in the course of debates in the House of Commons; unfortunately, the Prime Minister's reply that "Field Marshal Montgomery had no responsibility for any of the matters mentioned,"[4] was completely unsatisfactory and only reinforced the view that he was deliberately concealing his own role.

On the day of the German surrender in the west, Doenitz monitored public reaction and a report was compiled for the Admiral's consideration. It contained a description of the arrival of the British troops in Flensburg ("The forces are hardly regarded as the enemy"), and speculated on the future ("The reason for this can well be that the people more and more have the thought that Germany and the Western Powers . . . will cooperatively form a front against Bolshevism. There are already a few accounts of English-Russian clashes").[5]

The report, based on a broad sampling of opinions,[6] indicated wide-spread feeling that an Anglo-American war against the Soviet Union was imminent. Many German soldiers openly expressed a willingness to take up arms against the Russians again, and already one German radio broadcast from Hamburg requested all males from 16 to 45 years of age to report to the nearest army garrison.[7] The Germans would have been more convinced than ever if they had known the contents of a message from the British Prime Minister only the day before asking his Field Marshal in Germany why it was necessary to place captured German generals into prisoners of war camps.[8]

By this time, the Russians were openly showing their concern over the fact that Doenitz had not yet been arrested. Field Marshal Keitel, in Berlin to meet with the Russians, recorded a "private" conversation with Colonel General Serow, during which the Soviet General expressed some bewilderment about Doenitz's status at this date—it was May 8. What sort of position did the Admiral think he occupied, Serow asked Keitel? Did not the Germans know that there had been no arrangements made with Russian approval? Serow stressed the fact that Doenitz had been appointed by Hitler and owed his job to the Nazis.[9] It was clear from Serow's line of questioning that the Russians were already beginning to probe for the authority behind Doenitz's continued position. The Russian attitude could only be one of mistrust, for by no means did they see Doenitz as a mere administrative convenience to be used until order had been restored, but as a powerful ally if the West chose to use him.[10]

In fact, the Doenitz government was not exactly a powerless creature. The Grand Admiral, who now had the loyalty of the

Wehrmacht, had succeeded in moving millions of troops into northwestern Germany before final surrender. There is little question that Doenitz's primary motive was to rescue as many German soldiers and civilians as possible from Russian capture, but the sudden bonanza of two to two and a half million German prisoners of war delivered into Montgomery's hands was something that deserved serious thought.

By Montgomery's own calculations, he had accepted the surrender of about two and a half million German troops and an additional million refugees by May 5, 1945.[11] Schwerin von Krosigk, who praised the British Field Marshal as "fair" and the Americans as "hard" on capitulation terms, later revealed that about 1.25 million refugees made it to the west on German ships that the British allowed to pass without hindrance. Doenitz had ordered all German captains at sea to inform the British forces, whenever encountered, that the landings had already been authorized in the armistice talks, and if any ships were challenged, they were to fight their way ashore. Von Krosigk said this only happened once.[12] He insisted that many more German soldiers could have been rescued from the Russians if the Americans had acted as the British did between May 1 and May 8, 1945.[13]

In addition to the large concentration of troops in the Schleswig-Holstein and Lower Saxony regions, there was General Boehme's sizable force still intact in Norway when the war closed. As part of Montgomery's thrust to secure the western Baltic before the advancing Russians, Boehme had already been contacted via radio by the British to prepare for the early arrival of Allied representatives.[14]

In a move that later was to become the subject of Allied-Russian dispute, it was decided that "members of the German armed forces in Norway who surrendered effective 2301 8 May 45 would not be declared prisoners of war, but would be treated as disarmed military personnel."[15] A legal expert for the Allied Land Forces Norway noted the peculiarities of the decision by suggesting that it created "in international law an entirely new class of persons, viz, disarmed military personnel operating under a military organization and military law of a foreign country with only the top command and control changed by surrender. Such persons are not prisoners of war, nor are they displaced persons, but represent a class in between whose privileges . . . are not specified by . . . any international convention."[16]

General Boehme requested permission to retain military control over the Wehrmacht under his command in Norway and was given such authority in a special directive from the Allied Land Forces Norway. "A further interesting development is the distribution of staff responsibilities in respect to that body of persons. Normally, prisoners of war are an A/G-1 [Adjutant General] responsibility. However, in this operation C.A. [Civil Affairs] Legal Officers have been made responsible."[17]

It should be noted that as the Allies were taking in huge numbers of prisoners in the last days of the war, General Eisenhower had instructed all commanders to treat Germans who were surrendering just prior to the end of hostilities as disarmed enemy forces, and therefore distinct from prisoners of war. The peculiar legal preparations that were made for Boehme's troops were not applied generally, and Eisenhower's instructions did not relieve military commanders of their responsibility, nor allow it to be delegated. The special status offered German troops by the British authorities soon became the center of considerable controversy.

Meanwhile, Montgomery hastened to lay claim to Denmark for on May 5 Churchill had cabled the news that two Russian parachutists had already been spotted south of Copenhagen.[18] The German forces there had already begun the surrender to Montgomery preparatory to moving south into Germany.[19] The Danish island of Bornholm proved more difficult because the Russians succeeded in occupying it before the British could establish a foothold. Doenitz insisted that it was only through his efforts that the Russians did not take the island sooner, for the German Admiral had regarded the island as vital to his plan of moving as many German ships west and south as possible. He wrote, "In the first days of May, I advised Montgomery to occupy Bornholm as soon as possible, but the English came too late for on May 9, 1945, at 2:30 P.M., Bornhom was occupied by the Russians."[20]

In a continuing mood of pessimism, Churchill telegraphed Eden and Clement Attlee, both in San Francisco on the day the war ended in Europe, that growing Russian encroachment was a great danger and had to be confronted before the United States began withdrawing its armies, otherwise, he warned, there would be

nothing to prevent a third world war.[21] President Truman received
an equally foreboding communiqué as the Prime Minister cabled
him that now "the attention of our peoples will be occupied in
inflicting severities upon Germany, which is ruined and prostrate,
and it would be open to the Russians in a very short time to
advance if they chose to the waters of the North Sea and the
Atlantic."[22]

The Prime Minister had obviously already decided to retain
Doenitz in some semblance of power for as long as he could. He
readily acknowledged that the Grand Admiral might well be guilty
of war crimes, but one had to consider his degree of usefulness:
"Do you want to have a handle with which to manipulate this
conquered people," he wrote, "or just to have to thrust your
hands into an agitated ant heap?"[23] Such sentiments were not lost
upon the desperate remnants of Hitler's Germany and the assumption was made that Churchill had authorized Doenitz's government to continue after May 8, 1945.[24] During the period
following that date, Eisenhower's SHAEF headquarters was very
careful in the language used to describe Doenitz's status. A news
release from Paris referred to the "Flensburg group of Doenitz"
and stated that there had been no recognition of any form
extended and that the Admiral and his people were only being
used temporarily to aid the Allies.[25]

The situation quickly attracted wide attention, however, for
Doenitz had continued to authorize broadcasts from Flensburg to
the German people. One such broadcast on May 11 was made by
Field Marshal Busch, who informed his listeners that, on authority
from Doenitz and in cooperation with the British, he was taking
command of the German troops of the 21st Army Group located
in Schleswig-Holstein.[26] When later asked about such an agreement, Churchill replied, "Field Marshal Montgomery has . . .
reported to me that no arrangements of this kind were ever
discussed between him and Field Marshal von Busch and no
German armed forces were maintained in being after their unconditional surrender."[27] Montgomery's account of the incident is
somewhat different. He admitted that he intended to use the
existing German military organization to handle the large number
of prisoners and therefore, allowed the German command to
remain intact. He noted their eagerness to serve and be friendly,
and for which they expected to be regarded as British allies against

Russia. Montgomery said that he informed Busch on May 11 that "this attitude was entirely unacceptable," and threatened to replace him. After their talk, Montgomery said there was no further trouble.[28]

All of this was really part of a plan he had thought of in early April, Montgomery revealed. This had been thwarted by the British Foreign Office, however, so the Field Marshal finally decided to "work through the German command organization in the first instance, and to issue my orders regarding the disposal of the German forces to Field Marshal Busch, the German C.-in C. in N.W. Europe. He was to have his headquarters in Schleswig-Holstein. His Chief of Staff, General Kinzel, with a small staff and a team of liaison officers, would be at my main headquarters."[29] The plan, codenamed "Eclipse," divided the German forces into commands under German Generals Lindemann (Denmark), Blumentritt (between the Baltic and the Weser River), and Blaskowitz (from the Weser to Holland). The next step was to move all the German troops into the east and west coastline areas of Schleswig-Holstein and regions around Cuxhaven, Wilhelmshaven and Emden. Montgomery reasoned that "there was no other way of dealing with a million and a half prisoners; we could not put such a number into camps or P.O.W. cages."[30]

General de Guingand, Montgomery's Chief of Staff, estimated the number of German troops scheduled for the move at 1,419,000. In addition, there were 300,000 men in the Magdeburg area that became a part of the British command, thus bringing the figure to one and three quarter million German soldiers. "Besides this vast total, we also held on May 19 just under 200,000 German prisoners of war in camps in our . . . area," Guingand stated.[31] Three days before, Field Marshal Alexander had notified Prime Minister Churchill that he had collected an additional estimated one million German prisoners in the Villach-Klagenfurt area.[32] Thus, Great Britain had control of almost three million German troops in May 1945.

General de Guingand admitted that there was already some criticism of the manner in which Montgomery was using the German commanders and their staffs.[33] On May 17, Radio Moscow complained that Allied agreements to disarm the Germans were not being carried out and especially mentioned the continuance of the Doenitz government as a gross violation.[34] An

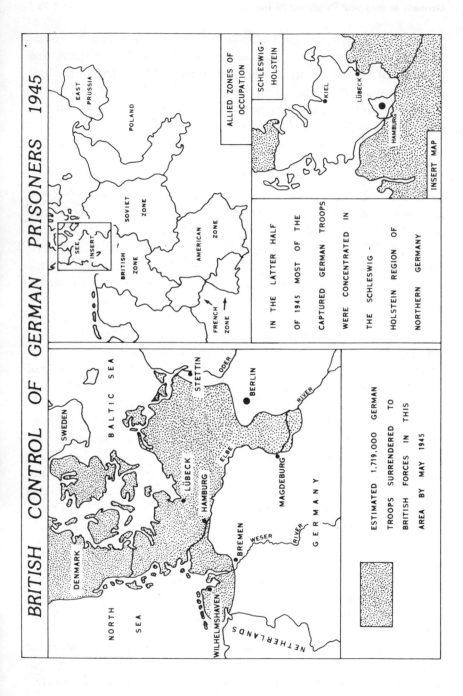

BRITISH CONTROL OF GERMAN PRISONERS 1945

NORTH SEA

BALTIC SEA

SWEDEN

DENMARK

NETHERLANDS

GERMANY

WILHELMSHAVEN

BREMEN

HAMBURG

LÜBECK

STETTIN

BERLIN

MAGDEBURG

WESER RIVER

ELBE

ODER

RIVER

ESTIMATED 1,719,000 GERMAN TROOPS SURRENDERED TO BRITISH FORCES IN THIS AREA BY MAY 1945

EAST PRUSSIA

POLAND

SOVIET ZONE

BRITISH ZONE

AMERICAN ZONE

FRENCH ZONE

SEE INSERT

ALLIED ZONES OF OCCUPATION

IN THE LATTER HALF OF 1945 MOST OF THE CAPTURED GERMAN TROOPS WERE CONCENTRATED IN THE SCHLESWIG - HOLSTEIN REGION OF NORTHERN GERMANY

SCHLESWIG-HOLSTEIN

KIEL

LÜBECK

HAMBURG

INSERT MAP

Allied newsman, recalling a visit to Flensburg at the time, wrote: "The war had been over two weeks, but we found officers and soldiers of the German Army and Luftwaffe wearing all their insignia, saluting each other, driving staff cars, and in general acting in such a way that I got the uncanny feeling that the war was still on and that I was somewhere behind German lines."[35]

In the meantime, it had come to the notice of officials in British home government that some British troops had been ordered to salute captured German officers. An inquiry was directed to the Secretary of State for War asking whether SHAEF had approved such an order and if the approval of Her Majesty's Government had also been secured? In reply, the War Office spokesman admitted that an interim order may have been given to a British division or so concerning the appropriateness of British soldiers saluting German officers under certain circumstances. However, the spokesman continued, it was no matter for future concern as General Eisenhower had already ordered that under no circumstances were any Allied troops to salute German officers or officials.[36]

There was present at Flensburg a SHAEF control party headed by the American General Lowell Rooks, which had arrived around May 12. Its purpose was to insure Wehrmacht compliance with Eisenhower's orders in the western areas of Germany.[37] Robert Murphy, General Eisenhower's civilian political adviser, who also went to Flensburg, regarded the question of whether or not a German government existed as particularly vexing. Since the surrender had been completed through Doenitz and his appointed representatives (both in Reims and Berlin), the Admiral's authority had obviously been recognized to some extent by the Allies. Arguments soon developed in Washington and London, however, over the validity of Doenitz's position, and the matter went to the Supreme Commander. Eisenhower decided to dispatch Murphy to Flensburg with instructions to investigate the problem commenting that the German Admiral was trying to sow the seeds of dissent between the Allies and Russia.[38]

Murphy reported that Doenitz never expected Germany to be without a government and assumed after the surrender that his own provisional government would be supported by the Allies. Murphy also confirmed Eisenhower's opinion that the Admiral was doing all he could to arouse the Allies against Russia.[39] Doenitz later remembered this talk with Murphy and said that he received the political advisor on May 18 for a discussion concerning his, Doenitz's, appointment as head of government. He was particularly struck by the American's lack of understanding about Russia, he wrote, and contrasted it with high praise for Churchill's astute insight into Soviet intentions.[40]

In recalling the same events of that last week of Doenitz's government, Schwerin von Krosigk definitely felt their days were numbered from mid-May on, for the Russians were complaining loudly in press and radio with sharp attacks on Doenitz and England for allowing him to remain. "We knew then," he wrote, "that we wouldn't be present [in Flensburg] much longer. The only thing we didn't know was the exact time and form our final act would take."[41] He continued that on the evening of the 17th, a Russian commission arrived and was quartered in a houseboat next to the "Patria," a Hamburg-American luxury ship that served as billets for the British staff. He said that the Russians immediately contacted the Germans, demanding copies of everything they had given the Western Allies and that while this was being duly accomplished by long and dreary visits aboard the houseboat, the Western Allies kept a close watch from next door.[42]

Marshal Zhukov wrote that at about this time Stalin called him in for a talk about the Flensburg situation and said, "While we have disarmed all the officers and men of the German Army and placed them in prisoner-of-war camps, the British are keeping the German troops in a state of combat readiness and establishing cooperation with them. . . . On Montgomery's instructions, the arms and material of the German troops are being collected and put in order." Stalin demanded that Doenitz and the German generals be arrested as soon as possible.[43]

Meanwhile, in the United States the War Department had already sent instructions to General Eisenhower to arrest Doenitz and his staff. A telegram from the U.S. State Department reflected some of the reaction that had begun to surface: "Public opinion in this country is becoming considerably aroused over this matter and criticism is not directed solely against the military authorities. The Department is unable to understand why Doenitz and his group were permitted for so many days freely to continue in their pretense of functioning as a government of Germany."[44]

Somewhat belatedly, some members of the House of Commons expressed similar puzzlement about the course of events at Flensburg. Churchill was asked directly if it had been by his express instructions that Montgomery refrained from arresting Doenitz and other Nazi leaders and allowed them to run a government at Flensburg? The Prime Minister's only reply was that he would give the question "very careful consideration."[45] A second House attempt was made to secure an explanation from Churchill when he was asked "whether it is not a fact that a great deal of concern was expressed by other Allied circles, including the Russians and Americans, regarding all that was going on in that area [Schleswig-Holstein] and the use to which Nazi leaders were being put? . . . is it not a fact that General Eisenhower had to overrule both Field Marshal Montgomery and the Prime Minister, and send a mission from S.H.A.E.F. to clear up the whole mob?" Again, Churchill's answer was brief, evasive and flippant as he suggested that there was enough material in the question to make several more.[46]

On May 23, 1945, the American Secretary of State was informed of the details of Doenitz's arrest: "This occurred at ten this morning. The Germans were informed that they might return under guard to their quarters to pack their effects. . . . Von Friedeburg . . . committed suicide by taking poison. The balance of the party departed from Flensburg this afternoon by 3 P.M. The arrest includes over 300 persons."[47] On the scene, Schwerin von Krosigk described the 23rd as a morning like all the rest with a gathering of ten-twelve people of Doenitz's staff preparing for the day's work, when suddenly heavily armed British soldiers pushed the doors open and a tank brigade surrounded the building. He said that none of the British or American officers with whom they had been working daily up to this time appeared; "we were held at machinegun point and ordered to undress completely. . . . Some suffered blows as we were relieved of numerous documents and valuables . . . then we stood for hours in the courtyard with our hands behind our necks. It was in this position that we were shown to a number of reporters and photographed. We were finally removed under heavy armored guard."[48] Thus ended the life of Doenitz's government after twenty-three days of existence, but it was not the end of Churchill's efforts to keep a grip on the Wehrmacht troops in Britain's hands.

The day after Doenitz's arrest, Lord Alan Brooke wrote, "This evening I went carefully through the Planner's report on the possibility of taking on Russia should troubles arise in our future discussions with her. We were instructed to carry out this investigation. The idea is, of course, fantastic and the chances of success quite impossible."[49] Churchill was not blind to the odds involved and he desperately wanted the backing of the United States in his stand, but even Montgomery recognized the growing reluctance of their American friends to become involved in a policy not of their making.[50]

The truth of the matter was that U.S. leaders were trying to put the brake on Churchill's plans while not being fully aware perhaps as to just what lengths the doughty Prime Minister was prepared to go. Harry Hopkins, preparing for a trip to Moscow in May amidst deteriorating U.S.-Russian relations, told a colleague that he was very "skeptical about Churchill" and felt strongly opposed to being maneuvered into a position of supporting British European policy against the Russians.[51]

Winston Churchill was not an ordinary man, however, and could not be dealt with by ordinary means. On May 27, the Prime Minister confided to General Ismay that the public would clamor for a quick return to prewar times, but it was not a time to demobilize. "I do not wish to be left alone with no troops at all and great Russian masses free to do whatever they choose in Europe. The above applies still more to the Air Forces, which would have to be our method of striking at the communications of the Russian armies should they decide to advance further than agreed."[52]

It was not just in Germany that Churchill feared Russian advance, but throughout central and south Europe as well. In discussing the situation in Yugoslavia with Alexander on May 30, the Prime Minister again expressed the fervent wish for U.S. support against the Communists, but insisted that Russia must be given the impression that force will be used to stop her if necessary. In line with this thinking, Field Marshal Alexander received instructions to prepare for a June showdown with Tito's forces if they did not retreat. Alan Brooke, in writing Alexander, expressed his doubts about such a conflict, feeling that a war against Yugoslavia would be very unpopular with British troops and would take considerable explaining. "I told the P.M.," he wrote, "and got a thick ear for my trouble! His attitude was typical and true to form, he refuses to face any facts that are in any way antagonistic to the plans he has in hand."[53]

Just how close was Winston Churchill to committing British forces—with German troops in support—to stopping any further Russian advance after May 8 or 9, 1945? On the basis of the argument already presented from available sources one would have to conclude that the Prime Minister was on the very brink, and that any urging from a responsible quarter would have been sufficient cause for a call to arms. There was already some precedent for doing so for Churchill "did not hesitate to oppose it [communism] whenever he had military force available. In November 1944, British troops were used to turn back Communist armed bands marching on Brussels; . . . in Athens in December, British opposition to seizure of power by the Greek Communists led to severe and prolonged fighting."[54] The apparent readiness with which Churchill proposed meeting the problem of Tito's threat in Yugoslavia was evidence that he had not lost his determination to use the utmost force when he thought it necessary.

Beset with growing doubts about U.S. support in an anti-Russian policy, Churchill had already ordered British commanders to end the war as far eastward as possible despite the existence of agreed-upon occupation areas. The idea was, of course, to hold territories for future bargaining purposes. In the push toward Vienna, Field Marshal Alexander had directed the 15th Army Group to occupy Austria with all possible speed "before there is a general German surrender or collapse on the Russian front so that we can use it to bargain with."[55] In late May and early June, Churchill constantly reiterated the theme of Russian aggression in no uncertain terms, and his language echoed his anxieties. In a note of June 2 to the Foreign Secretary, he wrote that whenever "these Bolsheviks think you are afraid of them, they will do whatever suits their lust and cruelty."[56] Again, only a few days later, he commented to Alexander that he was very disturbed about the "general attitude of the Russians, especially if they feel they have only war-wearied armies and trembling administrations in front of them."[57]

The question of Britain holding territory already marked for Russian occupation soon became something of a sore point with American authorities. In some ways, the Americans had already encountered the same problem with Berlin. There had been concern about the Allies beating the Russians to Berlin as early as 1943, but this did not present any difficulty when fixing occupation zones in 1944.[5][8] Churchill, however, knew these were political decisions and subject to wartime alterations and very definitely felt that any chance to beat the Russians to Berlin should be taken. The Prime Minister thought that Eisenhower should have ordered an advance on Germany's capital in late March and regarded the General's negative decision as a disaster.[59] The disappointment was aggravated by the manner in which Churchill received the news, for Eisenhower delivered his decision to make the attack eastward along a broad front—which did not include a thrust at Berlin—in a telegram to Stalin on March 28.[60] Indignant, Churchill took his complaint directly to Roosevelt, faulting the Supreme Commander for failing to consult the Combined Chiefs of Staff, and insisting that it was not too late to correct matters: the Soviets were "surprised and disconcerted by the rapid advance of the Allied armies in the west. . . . All this makes it the more important that we should join hands with the Russian armies as far to the east as possible and if circumstances allow, enter Berlin."[61]

The arguments have continued to rage on the pros and cons of Eisenhower's Berlin decision to stick strictly to the military demands of the situation as he perceived it and let the civilian leaders worry about the politics. The British, however, thought that once American forces had entered into Germany, they should have recognized that the conquest was accomplished and replaced their strategic aim with a political one.[62]

General Walter Bedell Smith rejected the viewpoint that Berlin could and should not have been taken by the Allies as well as Churchill's opinion that Western forces should have instantly advanced into areas already promised the Soviets. To have violated agreements, Smith warned, would have brought a terrible outcry against the United States, and "I personally feel sure we could not have stood our ground." He said he knew that Churchill felt very differently for shortly after the war the Prime Minister had told him that "our forces should remain for the time being where they were, deep in the Soviet zone. He felt it was a grave mistake . . . to withdraw . . . before definite agreements on various aspects of the occupation were reached with the Soviet Union."[63]

At a meeting of top U.S. officials in Washington, D.C. on June 6, 1945, the subject of British reluctance to surrender territory in the Russian zone was discussed. General John Hilldring, head of the War Department's Civil Affairs Division, expressed the view probably held by a number of participants, that the British were trying to turn SHAEF from its original purpose, namely to wage war against Germany, into an instrument for making political warfare against the Russians. Hilldring's opinion was supported by the American Chief of Staff, General George C. Marshall.[64]

Meanwhile, the Russians had already requested the withdrawal of Allied missions from Vienna by June 10. In a vain appeal, Churchill contacted Truman with the suggestion that the Allies stand firm: "If we give way in this matter," he wrote, "we must regard Austria as in the Sovietized half of Europe. . . . Berlin, of course, is so far completely Sovietized. Would it not be better to refuse to withdraw on the main European front until a settlement has been reached about Austria?"[65] Depressed by Truman's negative response, his gloom was deepened by the great physical presence of the Russian troops over central and eastern Europe and he was convinced that if it "took their fancy, they could march across the rest of Europe and drive us back into our island."[66]

While there were English statesmen who carried growing doubts as to the wisdom of Churchill's vehement anti-Russian policy, few dared speak openly against him.[67] This was not true of the Americans, however, for several persons have recorded their efforts to reason with the Prime Minister on the touchy issue of Soviet relations. General Smith told of such an attempt when reminding Churchill that both the American and British peoples had become convinced during the war years of the great value of Russian friendship and had strong hopes for the postwar world. To try to reverse that opinion, Smith cautioned, would be almost impossible.[68]

Another American official, Joseph E. Davies, described a talk with Winston Churchill in June 1945, during which the British leader expressed the fear of early U.S. withdrawal from Europe, leaving Great Britain to face the Soviets alone. Davies wrote that the Prime Minister's violent dislike of the Russians was so evident that he, Davies, suggested that perhaps Churchill wanted to tell the world that Great Britain should have supported Hitler. He also expressed the opinion that Russian awareness of Churchill's views and the belief that secret deals had been made between the Allies and the Germans accounted for their suspicious attitude toward the West.[69]

Unsuccessful in his attempts to convince U.S. leaders of the urgency of wringing concessions from the Soviets by all available means, Churchill still hoped that a final conference would bring needed support. In his proposal for the Potsdam Conference (July 17-August 2, 1945), which the Prime Minister had wanted a month earlier because the Allied armies would still have been in a strong position,[70] Churchill planned to win over the United States to possible future military commitments: "It was essential to do this . . . before the withdrawal of American troops left the British and Russians in single and unequal confrontation."[71]

The Russians were not unaware of Churchill's efforts to create such a military bloc against them. Zhukov wrote that when Stalin arrived in Berlin for the conference, he briefed the Soviet dictator on some of the details "where, just as before, we were coming up against our biggest difficulties in reaching understanding with the British side."[72]

The British too felt that Russia deliberately sought to misinterpret issues at Potsdam in lodging complaint after complaint against Great Britain. The Soviets charged that Britain was establishing military units in Italy composed of Russian citizens commanded by former German Wehrmacht officers. They also complained that the British military authorities had not disarmed 400,000 Germans in Norway.[73]

According to notes from the Russian account, it was at the ninth sitting on July 25 that Stalin accused Churchill of keeping the 400,000 armed Germans in Norway and asked the Prime Minister why.[74] Churchill expressed ignorance of the matter and promised an inquiry. Later, before the meeting adjourned, the Soviet delegation presented a memorandum placing their charges about the German troops in Norway in writing. This delivery prompted Churchill to remark, "But I can assure you that it is our intention to disarm those troops." Amidst general laughter, Stalin replied, "I have no doubt." However, Churchill had the last word by retorting, "We are not keeping them up our sleeve so as later to release them all of a sudden. I shall demand a report on this question at once."[75]

Meanwhile, the Allied Control Council for Germany began its meetings in Berlin (the first formal session started in July), and it was to be here in this body and its subcommittees that the

Russians continued to pursue their charges that Great Britain was holding their German troops in a state of war readiness.

NOTES

1. *F.R.U.S., 1945,* Vol. III, pp. 521 ff.
2. J. L. Gaddis, *The United States and the Origins of the Cold War,* p. 131.
3. *House of Commons Debates,* 5th Series, Vol. 535 (1954-55), pp. 1575-1576.
4. Loc. cit.
5. German Records, 18/866/5613541/T-77.
6. See A. L. Smith, Jr., "Life in wartime Germany," *The Public Opinion Quarterly,* V. 36 (Spring 1972), pp. 1-7.
7. German Records, 18/866/5613541/T-77.
8. W. Churchill, *Triumph and Tragedy,* p. 755.
9. German Records, 18/858/5604822/T-77.
10. W. Cornides, *Die Weltmaechte und Deutschland* (Tuebingen: R. Wunderlich, 1961), p. 39. In *The Year that Changed the World, 1945,* Brian Gardner wrote: "Both the Western Allies were reluctant to dismiss this powerless authority, believing it might be of use in enforcing law and order," pp. 172-73.
11. B. Montgomery, *Memoirs,* p. 319.
12. Article in *Christ und Welt,* Nr. 16, VIII Jahrgang (April 21, 1955).
13. Ibid., Nr. 17 (April 28, 1955).
14. *Keesing's Contemporary Archives* (London: Keesing's Publications, 1946), p. 7187.
15. H. Coles and A. K. Weinberg, *Civil Affairs,* p. 845.
16. Loc. cit.
17. Ibid.
18. Churchill, *Triumph and Tragedy,* p. 539.
19. J. Schultz, *Die Letzten 30 Tage* (Stuttgart: Steingrueben, 1951), p. 100.
20. Federal Republic of Germany, Militaergeschichtliches Forschungsamt, Freiburg im Breisgau, Karl Doenitz Collection, N236, Ltr. to Bidlingmaier, 14.5.66.
21. L. Woodward, *British Foreign Policy in the Second World War,* Vol. III (London: H.M.S.O., 1971), p. 575.
22. Ibid., p. 578.
23. Churchill, *Triumph and Tragedy,* p. 756.
24. Comment by Schwerin von Krosigk in *Christ und Welt,* Nr. 17 (April 28, 1955).
25. *Keesing's Archives,* May 16, 1945, p. 7213.
26. Loc. cit., and *House of Commons Debates,* 5th Series, Vol. 535 (1954-55), p. 773.
27. Ibid., p. 772.
28. Montgomery, *Memoirs,* p. 328.
29. Ibid., pp. 319-20.
30. Ibid., p. 321.
31. F. de Guingand, *Operation Victory* (London: Hodder and Stoughton, 1948), pp. 458-60.
32. Great Britain, Public Records Office, War Office, 214/42, "Papers of Field Marshal Alexander," File no. 17, Vol. III, Doc. 33.
33. F. de Guingand, *Operation Victory,* p. 458.

34. B. Meissner, *Russland, die Westmaechte und Deutschland* (Hamburg: H. H. Noelke, 1953), p. 57.

35. R. Hill, *Struggle for Germany* (New York: Harper and Brothers, 1947), p. 214.

36. *House of Commons Debates*, 5th Series, Vol. 310 (1944-45), p. 2647.

37. *F.R.U.S., 1945*, Vol. III, p. 781, fn. 84.

38. R. Murphy, *Diplomat Among Warriors*, pp. 271-72.

39. Ibid., pp. 272-73.

40. Karl Doenitz Collection, N236, Ltr. to Bidlingmaier, 14.5.66.

41. *Christ und Welt*, Nr. k8, VIII Jahrgang (May 5, 1955).

42. Loc. cit.

43. *The Memoirs of Marshal Zhukov*, p. 657.

44. *F.R.U.S., 1945*, Vol. III, pp. 782-83.

45. *House of Commons Debates*, 5th Series, Vol. 535 (1954-55), p. 773.

46. Ibid., pp. 1576-1577.

47. *F.R.U.S., 1945*, Vol. III, p. 783.

48. *Christ und Welt*, Nr. 18, VIII Jahrgang (May 5, 1955). Robert Murphy witnessed some of the drama, and wrote, "British military police made the arrests . . . they simultaneously 'liberated' some souvenirs for themselves." *Diplomat Among Warriors*, p. 273.

49. A. Bryant, *Triumph in the West*, pp. 357-58.

50. Montgomery, *Memoirs*, p. 338.

51. W. Millis and E. S. Duffield, eds., *The Forrestal Diaries* (Princeton, N.J.: Princeton University Press, 1951), p. 58. See also C. L. Mee, Jr., *Meeting at Potsdam* (New York: M. Evans, 1975), p. 27.

52. *Triumph and Tragedy*, p. 758. In his book on 1945, *The Year that Changed the World*, Brian Gardner charged that Churchill secretly slowed down British demobilization, p. 287.

53. "Papers of Field Marshal Alexander," File no. 17, Vol. III, Doc. 37.

54. G. F. Hudson, "The lessons of Yalta," in R. Divine, ed., *Causes and Consequences of World War II*, p. 229.

55. "Papers of Field Marshal Alexander," File no. 17, Vol. III, Doc. 41. See also H. Alexander, *The Alexander Memoirs*, 1940-45 (London: McGraw-Hill, 1962), p. 151.

56. Churchill, *Triumph and Tragedy*, pp. 759-60.

57. "Papers of Field Marshal Alexander," File no. 17, Vol. III, Doc. 35. See also G. Alperovitz, *Atomic Diplomacy: Hiroshima and Potsdam* (London: Secker & Warburg, 1966), p. 42.

58. J. L. Gaddis, *The United States and the Origins of the Cold War*, p. 76. See T. Sharp, *The Wartime Alliance and The Zonal Division of Germany* (Oxford: Clarendon, 1975).

59. M. P. Schoenfeld, *The War Ministry of Winston Churchill*, p. 243. For a discussion in support of Eisenhower's decision, see S. E. Ambrose, *Eisenhower and Berlin, 1945: The Decision to Halt on the Elbe* (New York: W. W. Norton, 1967).

60. *Triumph and Tragedy*, pp. 458 ff.

61. *F.R.U.S., 1945*, Vol. III, pp. 746-47.

62. B. Gardner, *1945*, pp. 146-47. See F. Loewenheim, H. D. Langley and M. Jones, eds., *Roosevelt and Churchill: Their Secret Wartime Correspondence* (New York: Saturday Review Press, 1975), p. 43.

63. W. B. Smith, *Eisenhower's Six Great Decisions*, pp. 221-23.

64. *Morgenthau Diary*, Vol. II (Washington, D.C.: U.S. Government Printing Office, 1967), pp. 1563-1564.

65. "Papers of Field Marshal Alexander," File no. 17, Vol. III, Doc. 40.

66. Bryant, *Triumph in the West*, p. 358.

67. H. Dalton, *The Fateful Years: Memoirs 1931-1945* (London: Frederick Muller, 1957), p. 457.

68. W. Smith, *Eisenhower's Six Great Decisions,* p. 223.

69. *F.R.U.S., The Conference of Berlin,* Vol. I (Washington, D.C.: U.S. Government Printing Office, 1960), pp. 68-77.

70. E. Davidson, *The Death and Life of Germany* (New York: Alfred A. Knopf, 1959), p. 65; and Churchill, *Triumph and Tragedy,* p. 599.

71. J. Wheeler-Bennett and A. Nichols, *The Semblance of Peace,* p. 293.

72. *The Memoirs of Marshal Zhukov,* p. 669.

73. L. Woodward, *British Foreign Policy in the Second World War,* Vol. III, p. 542. See Mee, *Meeting at Potsdam,* p. 182.

74. R. Beitzell, ed., *Teheran, Yalta, Potsdam, The Soviet Protocols* (Hattiesburg, Miss.: Academic International, 1970), p. 252.

75. Ibid., pp. 252-53.

Chapter 5

THE LIMITATIONS OF BRITAIN'S POWER

The first months of peace in Europe meant different things to each of the victors. The United States still faced a formidable foe in the Pacific, and the defeat of Germany meant that a full effort could now be concentrated upon Japan. In addition, America still anticipated a future of cooperative endeavor with the Soviet Union in meeting the immediate problems of a devastated central Europe. Of course, Great Britain and later Russia contributed to Japan's ultimate defeat, but both these nations had already expended their maximum effort against Germany. For Churchill and Stalin, the real power struggle was for the control of central Europe, and since that outcome had not yet been decided, the first months of peace meant time to try to gain that control.

Although a peace treaty with Germany had not materialized and border questions appeared vexatious, the real concern of Churchill—and soon Clement Attlee—was to convince the United States of the seriousness of the Russian menace. France, although now a full partner in Germany's occupation, was still weak and generally concerned with burdensome domestic problems. There-fore, Great Britain's position appeared even more fragile. President

Truman had already shown that he intended to follow the policies of Roosevelt, who had made it abundantly clear to Churchill during the war that American forces would not remain in Germany very long after its collapse.[1]

The months following Germany's collapse, the period that is really the beginning of the Cold War, "is dominated by the dialogue between Churchill and Stalin which opened with an exchange . . . on problems of Eastern Europe and closed with Stalin's retort to Churchill's Fulton, Missouri address in March 1946."[2] The ultimate step—war—was not taken, either by Churchill or Attlee, during those critical ten months from May 1945 to March 1946. Stalin made no overt attempt to push further into western Europe, and, most importantly, the support of the United States began to move in Churchill's direction. However, the period immediately following Germany's surrender was another question altogether, and although the British Labour party was in power, England's defense policies remained largely unchanged.[3]

Even before the war in Germany was over, the lines were drawn between Great Britain and Russia, and while British forces prepared for clashes with Communists in Yugoslavia and Austria, the real issue at stake was the control of Germany. Here was a huge land expanse that had recently been the most powerful nation in Europe and was now reduced to a dependent mass of humanity searching for food and shelter. Both Britain and Russia had long recognized the great value that would accrue to the country that could influence the reshaping of a German nation.

There was no question that as Churchill saw it, the most pressing task, short of war, was to prepare for a defensive war. Alan Brooke wrote that when news of the successful atomic bomb explosion reached them at the Potsdam Conference, Churchill immediately evaluated its future potential in international relations: "He was already seeing himself capable of eliminating all the Russian centers of industry . . . and dictating to Stalin!"[4]

In the summer of 1945, Churchill was in one of the most difficult periods of his political life. Officially, he was out of office and without the power of the state behind him, but given the support for his convictions in the British government, the rather open hostility toward Russia was little disguised by the new Labour administration. Generally, the people who helped make and implement policy in Germany as employees of the British government were still the conservative colonial administrators, army officers, aristocrats and civil servants who had been in these positions before Attlee's victory. In general, they disliked, mistrusted and made little effort to understand the Russians, and it was an open secret that many of these same people thought that a war with the Soviet Union was only a matter of time.[5] Given these conditions, the fate of the defeated German army was of tremendous importance.

In 1944, the British War Office had produced a working paper on "Policy of Post-War Employment of German Prisoners-of-War"[6] in anticipation of utilizing German POWs for labor. Recognizing some preconditions, it was agreed that German POWs could not be released and recalled again, nor could prisoners be taken after the end of hostilities. Therefore, it was essential to know Britain's labor needs well in advance and what portion of those needs could actually be filled by POWs. There were restrictions by virtue of the Geneva Convention that had to be observed, but, as the top secret memorandum noted, if German prisoners were controlled by their own officers and if a jurisdiction was created for this express purpose, the problem took on a different face: "This solution provides a fixed administrative code and does not confer Convention rights. . . . It might be necessary technically to declare them released from POW status in view of the Russian proposal now embodied in the Armistice terms."[7]

The document further explored the possibility of using German POW labor in the war against Japan, suggesting four approaches that might be used: (1) keeping the Germans in prisoner-of-war status; (2) allowing German POW formations to remain under the command of their own commanders; (3) discharging the German POWs and organizing them in a civilian corps; or (4) simply discharging the POWs and allowing them to return to their homes. It was noted that if approach number two was taken, there would probably be undesirable political consequences.[8] This was not elaborated upon.

Shortly after the war had ended, Montgomery complained to the War Office about the confused policy regarding German prisoners-of-war taken in the last days of hostilities. The problem was distinguishing between those Germans who were to be treated as prisoners-of-war and the huge number who surrendered at war's end and were held as disarmed enemy personnel. The War Office informed Montgomery that since the Geneva Convention restricted the use of POWs, it was permissible for British commanders to regard them simply as disarmed troops whenever deemed necessary.[9]

In early June 1945, Great Britain announced the formation of work battalions in Germany to be drawn from disarmed Wehrmacht personnel. The direction and control was to remain in the hands of British commanders and work would include mine clearance. In addition, the press release noted, British military installations would begin the use of displaced persons as guard personnel.[10]

Before Churchill had vacated office, he had requested the British Secretary for War to consider the use of some 128,000 Polish troops who had fought for Great Britain, for a "Corps of Occupation in some part of the British Zone. . . . The question of their recruitment from time to time requires further study," he wrote. "We need these men desperately, and I cannot see what the Russians have to say to it, any more than we are consulted by them when they deport a few hundred thousand people to Siberia."[11]

It had already come to public attention in Great Britain that armed Wehrmacht soldiers were being used in Germany by the British Army. The War Office admitted that there were about 20,000 Germans under arms: "They are used for guarding food dumps and other such purposes and so relieve British troops. They carry small arms only and a limited amount of ammunition. They have, of course, been submitted to the usual security procedure."[12] The question of uniforms had already been the subject of an Allied Control Council decision, which expressly forbade the wearing of any sort of uniform, but it was immediately and generally ignored because of the severe shortage of clothing. Somewhat later the Soviets did enforce the uniform ban, except for a cap without insignia.[13]

At the same time, Montgomery was protesting his own manpower shortage as a result of having to guard large numbers of prisoners-of-war and huge quantities of arms and ammunition.[14] The British Field Marshal agreed that the rapid discharge of

German POWs was proceeding well—about 12,000 men daily—but "to offset this, large numbers of fresh prisoners were arriving from Norway [June and July 1945] and the total number of German prisoners held in the British Zone now amounted to 1,850,000."[15]

It appears that for the most part, the United States knew little and cared less about the British manpower requirements and the use of German prisoners under their command, at least in the summer and early fall of 1945. It was generally assumed that the Geneva Convention would be observed, and there were combined Chiefs of Staff directives that provided guidelines.[16] There were some disquieting signs, however, for Marshal Zhukov was already protesting that Yalta decisions were being ignored in the Allied zones in respect to German demilitarization,[17] while Field Marshal Montgomery was observing that the rift with the Russians was growing ever wider.[18] Even Harry Hopkins, on a brief June visit to Germany, commented on the uneasy feeling he got "by suggestions I hear from some quarters that we do little or nothing to prevent the Germans from starting this business all over again."[19]

There is no doubt that Hopkins would have had his fears confirmed had he known of British efforts to reorganize some of the German troops they held in POW enclosures. Dr. Meier-Welcker, former Chief of the General Staff of the German 31st Army Corps (Corps Ems), remembered that after his forces had surrendered to the British and were in a holding area, he received a visit from some English officers: "It must have been in June-July, as the Chief of the General Staff had two visits from two British officers of the Army of the Rhine. In a meeting that was confidential he was asked if the troops of the Corps Ems were ready to fight against Russia and Japan?"[20] Between the months of June and September, the question of what happened to the millions of German prisoners in English hands is rather complex; it is significant, however, that the disbandment of the German POWs in the British zone continued as an issue into the autumn of 1945.

"Eclipse" called originally for about forty prisoner concentration areas in the British sector, but this was changed to four large areas instead, all in the northwestern coastal region of Germany, and all filled to capacity during May and June. The next operation, called "Barleycorn," planned for a massive processing and discharge program during the summer months, and succeeded in turning about a million Wehrmacht veterans back to civilian life by September.

The entire program was complicated by additional tens of thousands of foreign nationals—including Russians, Poles and Yugoslavs—who had to be documented and processed. Montgomery's deputy, General de Guingand, described the situation of displaced persons as a very difficult one, for there was a huge roving mass of people, estimated at almost a million, who were without organization or order, living off the land, stealing to eat, and creating serious problems. In view of the POWs, the displaced persons, a pending food shortage, and the responsibility to minister to hundreds of thousands of sick and wounded, it is little wonder that de Guingand wrote that "it is easy to see what a colossal task now faced us. Chaos everywhere, and the problems looked almost insoluable."[21]

Considering these conditions, it was understandable that most of the summer passed without complaint from the Russians about the status of the German prisoners under British control. At Allied Control Council meetings in August, the French again brought up the question of prohibiting former German soldiers from wearing uniforms, wishing the ban to be enforced. In voicing his objection, Montgomery stated that such an order would directly affect about two million men in the British zone. He pointed out that most of the men had no other clothing to use, and to dye existing clothing—as Eisenhower suggested—was simply too big a job. The British Field Marshal requested that the problem be left to the discretion of zone commanders. Zhukov expressed the opinion that Montgomery was exaggerating his problems for the Soviets had already largely completed the task in their zone, and lent his support to the French proposal. At the final meeting in August, the proposal was approved with the amendment that uniforms might be worn if dyed a different color.[22]

In mid-September, The London *Times* reported that in the past four months the German Wehrmacht had almost ceased to be: "Of the 2,250,000 prisoners taken on Field Marshal Montgomery's front, about 1,500,000 will before long have been discharged under such priorities as the 'barleycorn' and 'coal-shuttle' [exchange operation of POWs between the British and U.S. zones] operations for getting men back to the land and to the mines without loss of time. These are essentially soldiers whose homes are in the British and American zones of occupation."[23] While Germans in uniform were seen everywhere, the article continued, the British authorities were hastening with dye preparations. It noted that while Norway and Denmark were now cleared of German troops, there were still problems in Germany relating to discharge, which is "not without its delicate and complicated aspects."[24]

Evidently, one of the complications referred to the large number of German prisoners still housed in the open with winter approaching. Another was the many nationalities found among the POWs (over forty!), and especially those from central and eastern countries like Poland, Hungary, Yugoslavia and the Baltic, who did not want to be returned home. On certain levels of administration, British authorities retained "skeleton German staffs as a convenient medium for handling the great mass of prisoners in Schleswig-Holstein."[25] This aspect in particular was later to provide the basis for considerable comment and complaint, especially from the Soviets. As one observer put it, "Some colour was lent to their [Russian] suspicions by the British practice of leaving Wehrmacht personnel under the control of their officers pending release and demobilization."[26]

Meanwhile, at the Foreign Minister's Council London meeting in September, the American Secretary of State, James Byrnes, proposed to his Russian counterpart, Molotov, the possibility of a 25-year treaty guaranteeing the demilitarization of Germany. It was agreed that the Byrnes proposal was acceptable in principle, but needed additional study.[27] There was already general agreement on German disarmament incorporated in the Potsdam Conference deliberations, although no specific date for completion of that task had been set.[28] The prohibition of any form of military training, wearing of uniforms, insignia, saluting or display of flags had already been the subject of an OMGUS (Office of Military Government) directive in the U.S. zone on July 14, 1945.[29]

During the summer of 1945 there is little evidence of any Russian dissatisfaction toward the U.S. authorities in the American zone of occupation, and, in general, U.S.-Russian relations in Germany were still functioning fairly well. The same cannot be said for Russo-British relations, however, for in October, on a London trip, Montgomery confided to Prime Minister Attlee that cooperation with the Russians in Germany had become simply impossible. He insisted that it was time for the British to develop some strategy of their own and to stand fast in their present position.[30] Actually, the Field Marshal need not have worried much about developing strategy for very shortly, Russian charges against the British zone commander would provide the home government with more than enough raw data for a beginning.

The Russian charges against Great Britain, dealing with the maintenance of German troops under arms and training, had already surfaced in official quarters twice before a lengthy November memorandum was presented to the Allied Control Council. The question of armed German personnel in the British zone had first been raised in the Coordinating Committee (The Allied Deputy Military Governors) of the Control Council on September 17. On that date, during a discussion on disbanding the German forces, General Sokolovsky, the Soviet representative, took exception to the continued existence of what he said was armed German personnel in the British zone.[31]

Great Britain's member of the Coordinating Committee was General Brian Robertson, who formally replied to the Soviet complaint on October 26. Robertson expressed his concern over the misunderstandings that appeared to block agreement on a measure to prohibit military training of Germans, but confessed to an increasing pessimism on the whole matter. He noted that Sokolosky apparently objected to three specific activities going on in the British zone: (1) German crews serving under their own command aboard German vessels and wearing uniforms (without insignia); (2) German ex-naval personnel serving on mine-sweeping duty; and (3) ex-Wehrmacht personnel working for British authorities in administrative jobs. Robertson wrote that in each instance, Germans were serving the British aims, for it was convenient and less costly that way. Former Wehrmacht people were not armed and their uniforms were being replaced with civilian clothing as speedily as was possible, Robertson continued. By way of explanation, the British general stated that the Germans so used were "in fact prisoners of war, but technically we do not describe them as such because we do not wish to give them the status of prisoners of war under the International Convention since we wish to employ them on tasks which are not allowed in that Convention."[32]

Robertson's reply was not satisfactory, and a second Soviet rebuke came just a few days later when Marshal Zhukov personally spoke to the British general concerning a German language broadcast from London that had outlined the establishment of a new German army headquarters in Hamburg. Robertson assured the Marshal that the "broadcast was phrased in a misleading way, and I should like to put the correct details before you."[33] He then proceeded to deny specifics of the broadcast that *Wehrkreis* 10 had been reformed, stating that, in fact, it had been dissolved on October 14. He did admit, however, that some personnel had been kept intact together with other personnel from Army Group Mueller and Korps Witthof. It was correct that this body had been formed into an administrative structure under the German General Kramer. It was also true, Robertson continued, that this was located in Hamburg, and he carefully outlined its function as administering German hospital personnel, maintenance of communications networks, road repairs and other tasks helpful to the British command. Robertson defended Kramer as "an ardent anti-Nazi," and insisted that all the German personnel "is kept under constant review. I would emphasize that their only role is administrative. They are very strictly under British supervision. They are temporary in character and are retained solely to save work for British Staffs, pending final disbandment of all ex-Wehrmacht personnel."[34]

The Soviets completely ignored Robertson's two replies—Montgomery was in England—and continued to prepare formal charges for Control Council presentation. The long memorandum written in sharp terms and charging the British with numerous gross violations of the Potsdam Agreement was circulated to the Control Council on November 20 by Marshall Zhukov.

The Russian Marshal insisted that despite the Potsdam meeting, the British continued to organize and train German forces in their occupation zone. Zhukov's memorandum, dated November 19, was circulated to council members before the meeting, and as he later recalled, he felt great indignation that "to this day there exists a German Army Group," and he knew that Eisenhower was aware of the situation.[35] When the Marshal spoke of these events over Radio Moscow in December 1945, he made direct reference to the British command in Europe having begun the "betrayal" under orders from Prime Minister Winston Churchill.[36]

Zhukov's memorandum, submitted to the twelfth meeting of the Control Council, briefly outlined the existing Allied decisions to disarm the Germans since the war in Europe had ended, and emphasized the fact that in light of such agreements, there should be no German military units of any nature left on German soil. The Marshal did not reveal his exact sources of information for the charges, although he made reference to the foreign press and details made available to him through his own command. He stated without equivocation that there were German army, navy and air force "authorities" in the British zone of occupation.[37] Very specifically, the Soviet Marshal wrote that Army Group Mueller had not been dissolved, but simply renamed in October Army Group Nord with a field administration and staff containing a complement of departments and services (quartermaster, transport, officer personnel, etc.). In addition, Zhukov's memorandum continued, there were land, air and antiaircraft detachments with two corps groups (Stockhausen and Witthof) numbering over 100,000 men each![38]

On November 30, Field Marshal Montgomery stated before the Control Council that "I was astonished to receive from Marshal Zhukov his memorandum."[39] Montgomery expressed amazement that he should be so openly challenged by another zone commander. He admitted that from time to time "each of us should entertain some curiosity as to how . . . certain matters [are] being conducted in the other Zones," and that inquiries would be made, but an "open challenge of this nature is a rather different matter."[40] He wondered aloud why the Robertson replies had not been satisfactory and why neither letter had been answered. "I can only think," Montgomery said, "that his [Zhukov's] anxieties result firstly from the fact that we do not officially describe all these ex-Wehrmacht personnel as prisoners of war, and secondly, that we employ German staffs to administer them."[41]

The British Field Marshal indicated quite clearly that he felt Robertson's letters had been more than adequate as replies; however, he reiterated the major points of need for labor and desire to avoid convention restrictions again. He could not resist a barbed comment on Zhukov's "sources of information," by admitting that while he could not account for everything, he did wish council members to know that fifty Russian liaison officers had been in the British zone since August. They had come to his command, Montgomery explained, in what he assumed to be a friendly spirit and had been given a warm welcome. This had been extended despite the lack of reciprocity from the Soviet commander, but it was very obvious, Montgomery angrily noted, that his hospitality had been badly abused.[42]

In his November 20 memorandum, Zhukov had also stated that besides the corps groups, the British had created five German corps districts (in Hammer, Itzehoe, Neumünster-Rendsburg, Flensburg and Hamburg), as well as some twenty-five local military command districts scattered over the zone.[43] In addition, Zhukov continued, there was a German air district headquarters (II) with detachments of the 18th antiaircraft division, bomber squadrons, fighter squadrons and close-reconnaissance groups. The entire staff was at wartime strength and had a communications force of five regiments with tank units and a military hospital network (20,000 available beds). All of this, Zhukov charged, was supported by a German naval force masquerading as the German Trawler Service and a ground force in training in Schleswig-Holstein of approximately one million German soldiers.[44]

Although Montgomery said that he would not reply to Zhukov's memorandum in detail before the council until the charges were carefully checked, he did proceed "to point out a few of the more important misconceptions." In the first place, Montgomery stated, there were only 99,000 disarmed Germans in Stockhausen and the Witthof area was no longer in existence. As for the one million German soldiers that were supposed to be in Schleswig-Holstein, Montgomery scoffed at the figure. Exclusive of the personnel in Stockhausen, there were only 148,000 men left in the northern provinces of Germany, and, Montgomery emphatically stated, "There is no Army Group Headquarters in my Zone."[45] And, furthermore, he continued, since the group did not exist, neither could operative departments. As for the staff, this was kept for administrative reasons only and had no similarity to a wartime staff. Finally, the British Field Marshal absolutely denied the existence of German bomber, fighter, attack air force, or tank units in the British zone.[46]

Zhukov had raised the issue in his memorandum of foreign detachments under British authorities. By this, he meant foreign armed forces that had fought on the German side and at war's end took refuge in western Germany. Specifically, the Marshal claimed that there were 12,000 Hungarians, 3,200 Estonians, 21,000 Lithuanians and Latvians, and all were organized into military units with staffs and commanders. Finally, he wrote, "All the above mentioned [including the Germans] . . . receive [British] army maintenance. The personnel . . . wear badges and decorations. All ranks of the personnel carry on military duties. They receive promotion in their services and are allowed leave with pay and maintenance."[47] The Marshal closed with the suggestion that an inspection of the British zone be authorized by the Control Council as soon as possible.

Field Marshal Montgomery quickly dismissed the question of foreign nationals being held and trained in his zone by replying that Soviet authorities would not allow them (27,000 Hungarians in particular) transit through Austria: "Those people are a great embarrassment to me and I shall be only too glad when their disposal can be satisfactorily settled."[48] On the Soviet Marshal's suggestion of an investigative commission, Montgomery heartily agreed, providing of course, that it have the power to visit all zones and investigate all matters dealing with the administration of Germany. He especially made the point that this idea had been put forth by the American zone commander, General Lucius Clay.[49]

Clay's own description of the event remains rather general considering its importance. He remembered a comment by Montgomery after Zhukov's charges had been made: "We do not consider a helpless mass of Germans on an island in the Baltic as a perpetuation of the Wehrmacht," the British Field Marshal had said, "nor the small administrative staffs to do the work of administration a perpetuation of the German General Staff."[50] The American zone commander acknowledged, however, that the suspicions of the Russians certainly were aroused and that this definitely was not the end of it. He revealed that American authorities had not been unaware of British activities, but regarded their use of German personnel "as administratively helpful. However, we had urged . . . that these organizations be broken up to avoid any possible basis for Soviet protest."[51]

Later, Zhukov wrote that as Montgomery made the attempt to refute his charges, his "American colleague, General Clay, kept silent. He obviously knew about the British Premier's directive."[52] This was meant as a reference to Chruchill's instructions at war's end to Montgomery about standing fast against the Soviets. As one writer put it, "The Russians clearly entertained the suspicion that the British were keeping units of the German Army intact for possible future use against the Soviet Union."[53]

Montgomery's evaluation of the Russian stance was that while they were indeed very suspicious, Zhukov had been friendly toward him at the Control Council meetings. Nevertheless, the British Field Marshal felt that "a blunt reply" was in order and decided "that a heavy counter-attack must be launched against the Soviet delegation."[54] Montgomery's militant solution was plainly not accepted by all and sundry in the home government.

Since Zhukov had distributed his memorandum on November 20 to the Control Council, it meant that British governmental departments were already well-informed on the content of the document long before Montgomery's reply on the 30th. It still remained an issue that had not yet become public knowledge, however. The first reaction of the Foreign Office was to suggest to Montgomery's headquarters that Clay's recommendation should be pushed: "we felt that provided the scope of the proposed commission can be extended to include all four zones . . . there might be considerable advantage . . . as this would give us a valuable means of entry into the Russian zone . . . in case we wanted to lodge a complaint about something."[55]

The Foreign Office message was dispatched to Montgomery on the 23rd of November, and a War Office communication of the 26th revealed that news of Zhukov's charges was leaking out of official circles. The War Office telegram with handwritten notations suggesting that the news leakage "may well have been an 'official' one," but probably not until that very day, read in part, "There has been a leakage on the subject of Marshal Zhukov's protest to the British over their employment of German ex-Wehrmacht personnel." In view of this, it was decided that a press conference was the best strategy for the release of a statement revealing Zhukov's actions and that there would be no further news until proper discussions could be arranged.[56]

Shortly after the news was released, Montgomery cabled the Foreign Office that his every interest was to take a strong stand on the entire matter with "a heavy counterattack against [the] Russian delegation" at the council meeting on the 30th; he outlined his reply, and strongly endorsed the Clay proposal of an investigative commission.[57] Meanwhile, public interest in the whole affair had grown with reports like the Manchester *Guardian* account of November 30th from Hamburg: "The discovery of a German general and his entire staff masquerading as junior officers and other ranks is reported here today . . . security officers who checked through records of all Wehrmacht personnel made the discovery that the captain commanding the company was a lieutenant general, his lieutenants were brigadiers, the sergeants colonels, and the majors and privates other officers."[58] The military unit referred to was one of a number of German transport companies retained for aiding British personnel.

Soon after Montgomery's November 30th reply, a Foreign Office message reported on the meeting: Zhukov had agreed to table his memorandum, providing the Potsdam decisions were executed and the remainder of the Wehrmacht units disarmed. This must be speeded up, the Soviet Marshal declared, and proposed the establishment of a large commission drawn from all four zones to make an inspection. He did not object to a visit in his zone, but added that he saw no necessity for a permanent body or periodic visits as Montgomery had suggested. The American commander, General McNarney, "stated that he was very surprised at condition of Wehrmacht in British Zone and in particular at existence of Staff and HQ's. He gave his opinion that British had failed to carry out one of the provisions of the Potsdam agreement in this respect. He considered that Council has right to demand uniformity of action in all zones."[59] McNarney was also against the creation of a commission unless its powers were aimed at affairs of agreed importance only. These views were held by the French commander, General Koenig, as well. It was finally decided that the matter would be referred to a coordinating committee to investigate and report later.[60]

Meanwhile, Sir Arthur Street of the Foreign Office expressed the growing concern developing from Zhukov's charges: "Though no doubt it [Zhukov's memorandum] contains many absurdities and exaggerations," he wrote, ". . . I fear there is probably enough truth in the report of the staff and command structure of the undisbanded German forces in our zone to justify the sinister interpretation placed thereon by the Russians."[61] Street definitely felt that the British defense at the Control Council had not been terribly successful, "and General McNarney seems to have been particularly unhelpful to us on this, his first appearance at the Control Council."[62]

In Germany, the debate had moved to the Coordinating Committee for discussion since the Russians insisted this was the next step in handling the matter, rather than continued discussion at the Military Directorate level. Montgomery now requested of his own government that he should be relieved of the commitment of retaining 225,000 German military personnel marked for reparations labor in Great Britain, however, the Labour Ministry was reluctant. For a variety of reasons, including a lack of policy, the ministry did not wish the subject to be given any publicity, although the legality of such action was clear, deriving its authority from the surrender declaration. This created some problem for it was obvious that if the detention of some one-quarter million Germans could be explained as reparations labor, tensions would ease somewhat. In addition, the United States was anxiously requesting Foreign Office guidance for dealing with the press there.[63]

A statement was finally prepared for the American Secretary of State by the Foreign Office which summarized and defended the British position. Admittedly, there were some 700,000 undisbanded former German soldiers who were still wearing a uniform of sorts (without Nazi emblems, however) in the British zone, the United States was informed. Among that number were German naval crews, working parties, POWs still in the Schleswig-Holstein area to be discharged, and the 225,000 labor reserve destined for Great Britain. It was pointed out that in regard to the labor group, there probably would have been no question raised if England had simply had the adequate transport to get them out of Germany. It was agreed that some mistakes had been made:

It was clear that the British Element of the Control . . . [Council] feel that their position is somewhat vulnerable on this issue and that the Russians have scored some valid points. The Chief of Staff [General Robertson] has given orders for a drastic and immediate review of our attitude towards ex-Wehrmacht personnel. . . . It is clear that one of the mistakes made was the purely tactical one of using military terminology for the various surviving German units and staff. . . . The whole matter has of course been made more difficult by the fact that the Russians broadcast on 4 December over the Moscow Radio . . . Zhukov's memorandum.[64]

On December 6, *The Times'* military correspondent reported the Soviet charges and the existence of large numbers of ex-Wehrmacht personnel in the British zone. The final offensive of the British 21st Army Group was described and it was recalled that as it reached the Baltic, millions of German troops had been trapped there in the peninsulas. "It is in these areas that the wreckage of the Wehrmacht has remained."[65] The correspondent wrote that while large-scale demobilization had gone forward, the number of men remaining was still huge, and he indicated that a sizable proportion was from the lower ranks of the Waffen SS. The Soviet charges were, however, grossly exaggerated, he noted, for a British government release stated that two million German soldiers had already been released and the remaining 500,000 men would be processed for discharge as quickly as possible.[66] In the meantime, Montgomery was notified that he was to take no steps to discharge the 225,000 Germans desired for reparation labor until a ministerial decision had been made on the matter.[67]

In a rather incredibly written account to the Foreign Office (couched entirely in golfing parlance), Field Marshal Montgomery relayed his version of the Control Council discussion on November 30. He began by characterizing his reply to Zhukov as a drive "straight down the fairway. . . . McNarney . . . played the next shot. He was inclined to be hostile and when he had finished the ball was in the rough. It was then Koenig's turn and he . . . put the ball back on the fairway."[68] After these "remarks," Zhukov spoke again, which was described by Montgomery as the Soviet Marshal having "selected a club with great care and proceeded to try and put ball into deepest part of the rough," which meant the Russian proposal for an inspection commission. When this did not win immediate council approval, Montgomery suggested that Zhukov's "club slipped and the shot was a poor one. . . . I intervened and insisted playing next shot." That produced the Field Marshal's statement that "it seemed absurd to send a Commission of one hundred officers to check my statements. I then suggested proper answer was to refer the whole matter to the coordinating committee for full investigation by Military Directorate."[69]

As the "game" continued, so did Montgomery's description:

> This was a good shot and the ball was now back on the fairway and in a good lie. McNarney played a good spoon shot towards the green and Koenig took a Mashie and put ball on the green. We moved up to the green and by this time we were all laughing and joking about the match. It was clear that Zhukov was going to accept situation vide Para 5. But he obviously could not (not) hold out himself from that distance and he wanted to make me face up to an awkward Putt. He took out his Putter and played his shot which agreed more or less with Para 5. His ball finished some way from the hole and is not (not) lying dead. It is my shot next and we must try and hole out and it can be done if we study the line carefully. The next shot is a very important one. I have not (not) got exact club needed to hole out and will have to make it in shop and here I shall need your help as indicated in para 7.[70]

Reverting for a bit to more conventional expression, Montgomery wrote that he should get rid of the German staffs immediately which meant also the discharge of most German personnel. This amounted to a grand total of some 700,000 men and included the labor quota as well, Montgomery stated, requesting again that he be allowed to discharge the reparations group. "I must add," he closed, "that the Russians are deeply suspicious of our holding of 700,000 German troops and suspect our intentions."[71]

The entire affair had quickly mushroomed beyond the confines of the respective occupation commanders in Germany and the halls of the British Foreign Office. Not only had *Izvestia* carried a full account on December 4 beginning with Zhukov's memorandum, but the British Broadcasting Company followed suit two days later.[72] The glare of publicity combined with the lack of any rapid progress toward a mutually acceptable solution put the machinery of the Allied Control Council to its severest test yet.

There was grave concern in some diplomatic quarters that the council was in danger of imminent collapse, and that the Soviet challenge had been deliberately provocative. This latest development inspired a Foreign Office notation to the effect that "F. M. Montgomery's ball again appears to be lying in the rough."[73]

Working under increasing pressures, Montgomery instantly began the planning for a rapid disbandment of ex-Wehrmacht personnel under his command. He ordered a conference at the Rhine Headquarters of the British army and Operation "Clobber" was launched beginning December 10, which called for the complete discharge of German personnel by January 30.[74] Already the warning had been received from Sir A. Clark Kerr, Britain's Russian Ambassador, that the Soviets were "working up considerable indignation about the continued presence of German military formations in the British Zone. I think you should be prepared for them to raise the matter during the Moscow talks."[75]

Part of the "matter" was raised sooner than that, for a parliamentary question was asked on the 11th of December, inquiring about the results of the Berlin discussions. Specifically, the question posed was what had been decided—if anything—on the Russian proposal for inter-Allied inspection of German military organizations in the British zone. In addition, members wished to know the details on the existence of German military units, such as how many men there were, how many arms they possessed, and when they were to be finally disbanded. Parliament was informed by Montgomery's headquarters that the Soviet proposal had been referred to the Coordinating Committee. Further, disbandment was to proceed as quickly as possible with a total of some 520,000 Germans left to be discharged, none of whom were armed.[76]

· Shortly thereafter, the Foreign Office made it known that answers concerning the problems stemming from the Soviet charges had been provided the press and that these were considered adequate. There were no plans to give any further publicity to the affair, for it was not the practice to go outside official communiqués released by the four-power Control Council in Germany.[77] Meanwhile, the British cabinet was provided with an account of the deliberations of the Coordinating Committee. A secret message reported the December 17 meeting of the committee as a long one with the main discussion centering on the

Soviet charges. General Robertson had circulated a paper containing the details of Britain's plans for disbanding the ex-Wehrmacht staffs and personnel "to dispel the uneasiness expressed by Marshal Zhukov and General McNarney. . . . We did not admit that we had failed to fulfill the terms of the Potsdam Agreement."[78]

The major points of Robertson's paper provided the following statistical breakdown until that date: Wehrmacht discharged, 2,007,000; number still held in and outside Germany as "disarmed personnel," 293,000; held as prisoners of war, 111,000; sick, 90,000; service troops doing mine sweeping and other necessary tasks, 120,000; and German naval personnel, 42,000. This brought the grand total to 656,000 men of whom 126,000 were not German nationals. Robertson stated that by January 31, this number would be reduced to only the service troops of 120,000; the navy personnel of 42,000; and some 85,000 held in prisoner-of-war camps (in addition to 36,000 non-Germans). The transfer of non-Germans out of the British zone, specifically Hungarians and Rumanians, depended upon the Soviets granting transit facilities through Austria, Robertson noted.[79]

The Soviet response by General Sokolovsky agreed that the final figure named by Robertson was not objectionable, but as for the Hungarians and Rumanians, the transfer was for the British authorities to arrange. In addition, he said that the British were keeping about 100,000 citizens of the USSR out of the statistics cited and preventing their lawful return.[80]

A British Foreign Office report noted that throughout the discussions, loyal support had been received from the French delegation. There was specific reference that the American deputy, General Lucius Clay, badgered the British regularly, but did not do so to the Russian deputy, General Sokolovsky.[81] This was a sore point to General Robertson and his delegation for there were some rather hostile feelings toward Clay for not giving support against the Soviets as well as the feeling that "the Americans in general are most anxious to keep the Russians 'happy.' "[82] However, Sokolovsky appeared generally satisfied with the British presentation and the cabinet was informed that a "report will be presented to the Control Council on December 20, and we may hope that the Soviet complaint has now been disposed of."[83]

British "hope" was obviously a bit premature, for at the Control Council meeting on the 20th, the Soviets brought forth charges anew. As Sir W. Strang phrased it, "We were too optimistic in thinking that at the Coordinating Committee we had disposed of all Soviet complaints. . . . At today's meeting, Marshal Zhukov, while accepting the plan for disbandment . . . brought forward a new series of complaints."[84] The new charges, three in number, were: (1) the British were continuing to recruit Germans for the British army; (2) the commander of Polish troops in the British zone was recruiting fresh Polish personnel (Zhukov made clear that his objection was not to the presence of Polish troops who had fought on the Allied side against the Germans; however, he wondered about their maintenance since they were not under the control of the Warsaw government); and (3) the 36,000 non-Germans had no business being kept in any sort of formation, and they (Poles, Balts, Hungarians and Rumanians) should be returned to their respective countries or at least be disbanded in the British zone.[85]

Interestingly, the American version of the meeting differed somewhat from that of the British. The American description characterized the opening talks as "a heated flare-up in discussion of the Coordinating Committee's report on German units in the British Zone."[86] The American report also noted that Zhukov had expressed a willingness to accept the disbanded non-German personnel into his zone; he had, however, received no information from the British about them nor their desire not to return to their homelands.[87] This comment was not in the British Foreign Office report prepared for cabinet distribution or elsewhere.[88]

In relating Montgomery's reaction to Zhukov's new complaints, the Foreign Office report stated: "As regards the first, Field Marshal Montgomery pinned Marshal Zhokov down . . . then gave a categorical denial. . . . As regards the second and third points, Field Marshal Montgomery said that he would consider what Marshal Zhukov had said."[89] The United States' State Department provided a different view here as well, noting that Montgomery asked, after he had agreed to "consider" Zhukov's comments, "outright that the Marshal confirm that he had said that the British authorities were enlisting Germans in the British Army." Zhukov did, and proceeded to state that the Germans being recruited were former armored personnel, aviators, ground crews, engineers, chauffeurs, and naval people, and that the cities used for recruitment were Hamburg, Kiel, Luebeck and Muenster. The British Field Marshal retorted that this was all untrue.[90]

On the issue of British recruitment of Germans into their army, Zhukov was to agree that this was not the case; he insisted that there was some misunderstanding, for he had not said recruitment "into the British Army."[91] Presumably, he meant the recruitment of an army of Germans. However, he also commented further on the question of Polish forces in the British zone by repeating the view that since Great Britain had extended recognition to the Polish government, a British command should not contain Polish troops who did not owe allegiance to the Polish government. Montgomery replied that this was not a matter for Control Council discussion, and refused further debate.[92]

Meanwhile, a creation of the Potsdam Conference, the Council of Foreign Ministers, had convened in Moscow in December where the U.S, British and Russian delegations attempted to resolve mutual problems. Although the Moscow meeting was focused upon a variety of issues that had remained unfinished in the wake of the Potsdam Conference, the British delegation decided to raise the current controversy raging in the Allied Control Council. The Soviet Foreign Minister had already alluded to the matter in informal discussion, and the British response was resentment at the doubt cast on Field Marshal Montgomery's veracity. On December 24, the British proposed that Montgomery's suggestion for a commission to visit all four zones be accepted; however, "the following day, Molotov said that he had received a letter from Marshal Zhukov which stated that the matter had been cleared up . . . and in consequence, the Soviet delegation wished to withdraw their proposal that a Commission of Investigation should be set up."[93] The British continued to press for Montgomery's suggestion, but privately agreed "that nothing is to be gained by further discussion [with the Soviets]."[94]

A War Office note of December 28 closed the year with the gross understatement that "what acute difficulties we are now having with the Russians in Germany [come] precisely because so many undischarged German troops have the status of 'disarmed personnel,' and not that of prisoners of war."[95] So ended 1945.

NOTES

1. *Foreign Relations of the United States, The Conferences at Malta and Yalta* (Washington, D.C.: U.S. Government Printing Office, 1955), p. 286.

2. J. P. Morray, *From Yalta to Disarmament: Cold War Debate* (New York: MR Press, 1961), p. 10.

3. C. J. Bartlett, *The Long Retreat: A Short History of British Defense Policy, 1945-1970*, p. 12.

4. A. Bryant, *Triumph in the West*, p. 364. See M. J. Sherwin, *A World Destroyed: The Atomic Bomb and The Grand Alliance* (New York: Alfred A. Knopf, 1973), pp. 83-84.

5. R. Hill, *Struggle for Germany*, pp. 212-13.

6. Great Britain, Public Records Office, War Office, 32/11132.

7. Ibid., Doc. 1A. See also Article 19, "Additional Requirements to be imposed on Germany," derived from the Surrender Declaration.

8. Ibid., Doc. 3A.

9. Ibid., Doc. 187A.

10. F. Kopp, *Chronik der Wiederbewaffnung in Deutschland* (Cologne: Markus, 1958), June 8, 1945, pp. 26-27.

11. W. Churchill, *Triumph and Tragedy*, p. 759.

12. *House of Commons Debates*, 5th Series, CCCXI, p. 1084.

13. J. P. Nettl, *The Eastern Zone and Soviet Policy in Germany, 1945-1950* (London: Oxford University Press, 1951), p. 69.

14. While Montgomery was requesting permission to destroy German weapons, Churchill was writing General Ismay: "What is being done with German rifles? . . . if possible, at least a couple of million should be preserved for Britain." *Triumph and Tragedy*, p. 765.

15. Montgomery, *Memoirs*, p. 350.

16. See *Morgenthau Diary*, pp. 1306-1307. According to the plan that dealt with the disbandment of the German army, "Eclipse," Allied zone commanders were authorized to use PW labor for a variety of necessary jobs.

17. *The Memoirs of Marshal Zhukov*, p. 664.

18. Montgomery, *Memoirs*, p. 345.

19. R. Sherwood, *Roosevelt and Hopkins* (New York: Bantam, 1948), Vol. 2, p. 572.

20. Letter to author from Dr. Brausch, June 18, 1973, containing affidavit from Dr. Hans Meier-Welcker. Meier-Welcker served in the German Army 1925-1945. From 1945 to 1947 he was in a British prisoner-of-war camp. He served as an advisor to the West German Defense Ministry 1952-1956 and from 1957 as department head at the Military History Research Office at Freiburg. Dr. Meier-Welcker has published extensively in the field of German military history.

21. Guingand, *Operation Victory*, pp. 460-61.

22. *F.R.U.S., 1945*, Vol. III, pp. 832-34.

23. September 13, 1945.

24. Loc. cit.

25. Loc. cit.

26. M. Balfour and J. Mair, *Four-Power Control in Germany and Austria, 1945-1946* (New York: Oxford University Press, 1956), p. 162.

27. See J. Byrnes, *Speaking Frankly* (New York: Harpers, 1947), p. 100.

28. United States, Department of State, *Occupation of Germany, Policy and Progress, 1945-46* (Washington, D.C.: U.S. Government Printing Office, 1947), pp. 90-91.

29. Ibid., p. 92.

30. Montgomery, *Memoirs,* p. 357.

31. Great Britain, Public Records Office, Foreign Office Doc. 371/46775/C9272. Hereafter cited as F.O., doc., piece, and reg. no.

32. Loc. cit.

33. Loc. cit.

34. Loc. cit.

35. *The Memoirs of Marshal Zhukov,* pp. 679-80.

36. *The Times* (London), December 17, 1954, quoting *Pravda.*

37. Great Britain, F.O., 371/46775/C9272.

38. Loc. cit.

39. Loc. cit.

40. Loc. cit.

41. Loc. cit.

42. Loc. cit.

43. The English translation of Zhukov's memorandum listed the locations as Pinneberg, Zegeberg, Luebeck, Lauenberg, Iterzen, Herkerkirchen, Beringstaedt, Itzehoe, Elmshorn, Schleswig, Ekkern-Ferde, Huzum, Westerland, Regensburg, Heibe, Marne, Wesselburen, Henstaedt, Meldorf, and Albersdorf. In his *Memoirs,* however, there is the correct spelling of Segeberg (Bad), Husum, and Ekernfoerde. Henstaedt is incorrectly spelled Hanstadt, and the place name of Wenzburg is added to the list. See p. 679.

Some of the above place names are difficult—if not impossible—to find. According to the Deutsche Bundespost there exists a Bad Segeberg, Herkersdorf, Kirchen (no Herkerkirchen), Heide (no Heibe), and Wittorf (no Witthof). Iterzen and Wenzburg or possible substitutes could not be found. Either the missing names are typing errors or have disappeared since 1945.

44. G.B., F.O., 371/46775/C9272.

45. Loc. cit.

46. Loc. cit.

47. Loc. cit.

48. Loc. cit.

49. Loc. cit. Clay had made the suggestion to the Control Council during Montgomery's absence.

50. L. D. Clay, *Decision in Germany* (New York: Doubleday, 1950), p. 112.

51. Ibid., p. 128.

52. *The Memoirs of Marshal Zhukov,* p. 665.

53. R. Hill, *Struggle for Germany,* p. 217.

54. Montgomery, *Memoirs,* pp. 361-62.

55. G.B., F.O., 371/46775/C8792.

56. Ibid., C9001.

57. Ibid., C8987.

58. Manchester *Guardian,* November 11, 1945.

59. G.B., F.O., 371/46775/C9003.

60. Loc. cit.

61. Ibid., C8987.

62. Loc. cit. McNarney replaced Eisenhower in November 1945.

63. Ibid., C9272

64. Loc. cit.

65. *The Times* (London), December 6, 1945.

66. Loc. cit.

67. G.B., F.O., 371/46775/C9272.

68. Ibid., C9141.

69. Loc. cit.
70. Loc. cit.
71. Loc. cit.
72. Ibid., C9177 and C9244.
73. Ibid., C9177.
74. Montgomery, *Memoirs,* p. 363. "Clobber," last of the British discharge operations for the German army, followed "Trek," the late summer movement of German
soldiers from Schleswig-Holstein into winter quarters, and, "Trickle," the fall-winter
discharge operation of some 350,000 men.
75. G.B., F.O., 371/46776/C9509.
76. Ibid., C9603.
77. Ibid., C9657.
78. Ibid., C9668.
79. Ibid., C9855.
80. Loc. cit.
81. Ibid., C9668.
82. Loc. cit.
83. Loc. cit.
84. Ibid., C9857.
85. Loc. cit.
86. *F.R.U.S., 1945,* Vol. III, p. 859.
87. Loc. cit.
88. G.B., F.O., 371/46776/C9857.
89. Loc. cit.
90. *F.R.U.S., 1945,* Vol. III, p. 860.
91. F.O., C9857.
92. Loc. cit.
93. Ibid., C9979.
94. Loc. cit.
95. G.B., W.O., 32/11132 (239A).

Chapter 6

THE LINES ARE DRAWN

While it was obvious that the multitude of issues relating to German disarmament that divided the wartime Allies in 1945 constituted only a small portion of the growing differences, the significance rested on the basic fact that Germany presented a mutual problem that could not be debated long distance. The nations' military and civilian representatives were compelled to attempt cooperative action on problems that reflected widely divergent proposals for solution, and Germany was the meeting ground. "In the field of foreign policy, which affected all our history . . . and the hopes of peace in the world," wrote one member of the British Parliament, "the principal problem was that of our relations with the U.S.S.R. and of our attitude to that country in connection with Germany."[1]

At the second Council of Foreign Ministers' meeting in Moscow (December 16-26, 1945), the American Secretary of State Byrnes proposed a German disarmament treaty of twenty-five years. This was obviously in response to the growing rift over the situation in Germany that dominated Allied council meetings. Secretary Byrnes spoke directly to Stalin in suggesting the treaty and indicated the readiness of the State Department to provide a working draft. By all accounts, the Soviet dictator appeared enthusiastic about the idea.[2]

By February 1946, the draft was ready for presentation to Great Britain, France, and the USSR. The proposal called for a cooperative commitment to German disarmament for a twenty-five year period, and inspection duties were to be vested in a four-power Control Council. The Russian Foreign Minister, however, indicated that the Byrnes draft provided insufficient detail. In addition, Molotov thought a forty year treaty period more appropriate than twenty-five years.[3] But the Russian raised a more immediate problem—his country's grave dissatisfaction with the present state of German disarmament in the western zones. When Byrnes insisted that the proposed treaty was the important feature because it provided the future basis for permanent security, Molotov returned to his earlier position that "such a treaty was useless in the absence of any immediate action to disarm Germany."[4] Shortly after this, Molotov repeated his charges in a radio broadcast from Moscow, saying in part, "Is it possible, for example, to overlook such facts when, let us say, hundreds of thousands of German troops of the defeated German army are kept, in one way or another, inside the occupation area of our ally?"[5]

It seems clear that while the United States proposed the German disarmament treaty, some of the impetus had come from the worsening Russo-British relations. Molotov's refusal to debate the treaty draft in good faith was definitely related to the Russian view that satisfactory disarmament measures had not already been taken against the Germans. Most specifically, former German army personnel under British control was the precise language of Molotov's Moscow broadcast.

These very serious statements were not lost upon the British government, and considerable publicity was suddenly devoted to the details of disbanding the German Wehrmacht. In late February, *The Times* stated that a senior British officer (unnamed) had provided recent information on disbanding the remainder of the German army: as of February first, the actual number of former German soldiers still in British hands was 360,000. Some 37,000 men were in concentrated areas, but only 9,000 of this number were German; the rest were Austrians and Hungarians with transport problems caused by the failure of Russia to provide proper exit documents. Finally, ten of the thirteen German administrative staffs had been dissolved with the remaining three due for dissolution soon.[6] A few days later, there appeared a long article entitled "Last of the Wehrmacht,"[7] which assured the British reading public that the task of disbanding the once powerful German army was almost complete. Reviewing the final operation, codenamed "Clobber," it was stated that within the past two months some 272,000 Germans had been discharged into civilian life and another 11,000 stood ready for release. This left 110,000 German POWs who could not be released for security reasons. Approximately 134,000 ex-Wehrmacht personnel were employed in the British zone, the article continued, "as staffs . . . supervising disbandment under British control; *Dienstgruppen,* the service groups used to eke out British manpower; and on mine clearance in German coastal waters. The disbandment of non-Germans has been slower; only 15,000 of the 126,000 held in December have been sent home."[8]

In his earlier radio broadcast, Molotov had made specific reference to the non-Germans remaining under British authority, especially the "thousands of troops of the Polish Facist General Anders, who is known for his hatred of the Soviet Union," as well as "a Russian 'White' infantry regiment which, during the war, was under Hitler's orders."[9] In partial reply, *The Times* article of February 26 noted that while some eighteen nationalities were represented among the non-Germans in the British zone who had served in Hitler's Wehrmacht, in particular the Poles, Hungarians and Russians did not wish to return home. Incidentally, the camps in which they resided were manned mostly by German staffs.[10] The article concluded with the interesting information that Germans serving in the *Dienstgruppen* formations were paid according to their former Wehrmacht rank, and that wives received a straight monthly allotment of sixty Reichsmarks if they resided in the British zone.[11]

The previous November, the occupying powers had agreed to a directive (Control Council Directive No. 18) setting specific guidelines for the dissolution of the German army.[12] The document allowed for considerable latitude on the part of each Allied commander in determining his nation's need for German labor, retaining security suspects in detention, etc., in the general process of disbanding the Wehrmacht. General agreement was attained on several specific points, however: each German individual was to be discharged into the zone that was his former home (a single discharge form was supposed to be used by all four zone authorities); non-Germans were to be returned to their respective governments as quickly as possible;[13] and German prisoners held outside Germany were to be returned eventually to their homes and demobilized. These guidelines appeared clear enough in terms of implementing existing agreement on the destruction of the Wehrmacht, while at the same time providing maximum use of German prisoners of war for labor abroad. That was obviously the intent of the directive, and since the Russian complaints—coming almost at the same time as the issuance of the directive—were aimed at British maintenance of a German fighting force within their zone, it can only be concluded that the occupying powers wished to give general approval to the keeping of POWs in their respective countries.[14]

The fact that Britain established the German *Dienstgruppen* in June of 1945, and continued to build their strength into 1946[15] was not in the spirit of Allied intent as expressed by the Potsdam Declaration and subsequent directives of the Allied Control Council for Germany. Additional suspicions were created by the fact that a significant proportion of the *Dienstgruppen* came from prisoners-of-war whose previous residences were on the other side of the Oder-Neisse Line or in the Soviet zone of occupation.[16]

The magnitude of the real issues at stake in the British-Soviet bickering in Germany and elsewhere suddenly became clear to the world on March 5, 1946. On that date, Winston Churchill spoke before an audience (including President Truman) at Westminster College in Fulton, Missouri, outlining his views on the differences that had developed between the former allies. It was premature, however, to include American feeling as synonymous with the British, for Churchill's words came as a profound shock to many people in the United States: "Uncertainty and unwillingness to join definitely in a coalition against Russia continued to exist among Americans for several months to come. . . . The real hardening of American opinion against Russia did not come until 1947 and 1948."[17]

The continued importance in England of Churchill's influence in foreign affairs should have been no surprise, for all the leaders of British Labour had lived and worked under Churchill during the war years and had absorbed much of his anti-Soviet bias. In fact, a significant portion of the Labour leadership had favored a continuation of Churchill's government until Japan was defeated (anticipated for 1946).[18] Clearly though, not all Labourites shared the former Prime Minister's views, for one member of Parliament at the time of the Fulton speech, Denis N. Pritt, wrote that "Churchill, now a private citizen, but still possessing prestige which made his international utterances of the greatest importance—so much indeed that it would have been wise and helpful from the point of view of the government of his country if he had refrained from such utterances. . . . The speech [at Fulton] was quite clearly an appeal for . . . [an] Anglo-American military alliance directed against the U.S.S.R."[19]

Churchill's talk that March day quickly became known for a sentence that ran: "From Stettin in the Baltic to Trieste in the Adriatic, an iron curtain has descended across the Continent."[20] Although the elderly statesman, now over 70, made reference to the close wartime relationship between himself and Stalin, as well as great admiration for the Russian people, he quickly moved toward his intended theme. Despite the great struggle recently concluded against Germany, Churchill spoke of a new danger threatening the world—communism. He touched upon the critical areas of the world where the future of freely elected governments was hanging in the balance. "Except in the British Commonwealth and in the United States," he told a rapt audience, "the Communist parties or fifth columns constitute a growing challenge and peril to Christian civilization."[21] Warming to his subject, Churchill rejected any possibility of creating a balance of power that would be respected by the Soviets; instead the old leader called for an alliance of an all-encompassing nature between the United States and the British Commonwealth. "From what I have seen of our Russian friends," he commented, "I am convinced that there is nothing they admire so much as strength, and there is nothing for which they have less respect than for military weakness."[22]

While press reaction varied somewhat in the Western world, certain facts appeared indisputable: Churchill, while proclaiming his status as a private citizen in calling for a powerful alliance, was not an ordinary individual, and the very presence of the American President meant that an even greater importance was attached to the speech. Interestingly, the former Prime Minister's proposals were not fully supported at home, and Attlee refused to allow debate on a motion raised in the House of Commons signed by over one hundred members, condemning Churchill's Fulton speech.[23]

Reaction from the Soviet Union was expressed by Stalin himself in a public broadcast that damned his wartime partner for the capitalist he was. How, Stalin asked, "can one reconcile such a statement [of expressed friendship] by Mr. Churchill with his set up for war against the Soviet Union? . . . [and] a new military expedition against eastern Europe."[24]

If there had been any doubts before about the cooperation among the wartime allies continuing into the postwar period, this should have confirmed them. While there is no general agreement by Cold War historians about the beginning, the events just related quite clearly indicate an emerging hostility between Great Britain and Russia before the United States was fully involved. British public opinion changed to hostility toward Russia in 1945-46, and this was definitely before U.S. opinion began to harden in that direction.[25]

During the crucial interval from war's end in 1945 to 1947, when the United States began to fully assume the mantle of British responsibilities, England had already abandoned all expectations of cooperation with the Soviet Union. Not only had Churchill shown a willingness to use arms against the Russians—with German help—in May 1945, but had, of course, already committed British troops against Communist forces in Greece before the war had ended. This he proudly referred to in his Fulton speech, when noting the Soviet domination of central Europe: "Athens alone with its immortal glories, is free to decide its future at an election."[26]

What had been occurring in those postwar months in Europe, and specifically in Germany, was a transformation of the British forces from an occupation army in a defeated nation to a defense structure—with the possibility of German support, if need be—for the West. Despite a rapid weakening of forces after 1945, the British army still was charged with the mission of Western defense by the nation's leaders. Was it true, asked one military historian,

that during this interval, when America was not yet totally committed to the Cold War struggle, that "the British Army of the
Rhine trained and prepared for a major defensive war?"[2 7]

Obviously, the Soviets thought so, and while international
diplomacy was still a viable function with the continued frequent
meetings of the Council of Foreign Ministers, the German situation remained a central question. At the Paris session of the
foreign ministers in April-May 1946, it was apparent that in the
aftermath of Churchill's Fulton speech, the Russians were convinced of the formation of a U.S.-British coalition that would
present a united front on all mutual problems with the USSR.
Summarizing the Soviet stand at the Paris meeting, Molotov explained to the Western press that Mr. Byrnes had erred in thinking
that Stalin had approved the U.S. Secretary's treaty proposal for
Germany the previous December. At that time, Molotov stated,
there had been only a brief exchange of opinions, and since Byrnes
had not yet even drafted a treaty, it had not been possible for
Stalin to give any approval. However, Molotov continued, the
problem was that the draft treaty, later submitted by Byrnes,
disregarded the important decisions already made by the Allies in
regard to Germany, and might "lead to a relaxation of inter-allied
control aimed at preventing a resurgence of German aggression."[2 8] Much of what the U.S. Secretary had proposed, Molotov
suggested, was pretty academic anyway, for such a treaty could
only come into force after a peace treaty was concluded with
Germany, and since that country did not even have the beginnings
of a government, everything else appeared quite distant at the
moment. Therefore, Mr. Molotov had a more practical proposal to
put forth (one which the Soviet delegation at Paris had already
offered)—to form a body with the object of immediate inspection
into the "occupation zones of Germany [to see] just how the
disarmament of the German armed forces had been carried out in
practice in the year since Germany's surrender."[2 9] Quite clearly,
the Soviet maneuver was to sidestep Byrnes' treaty proposal and
use the initiative to draw Western leaders directly back to their
complaints lodged against the British the previous November. The
action made it abundantly plain that the Russians remained
unconvinced of any British progress toward disarming the Germans in their zone.

The grave implications of the Russian charges were not lost upon political observers. Expressing much of the concern of his fellow journalists, Walter Lippmann, recently returned from Europe, wrote two lengthy articles on the subject in May 1946.[30] Lippmann indicated that he had access to many responsible individuals in Europe on his trip, and began his report with a most depressing and startling statement: "The most important conclusion I have to report is, I am sure, indisputable. It is that all European governments, all parties and all leading men are acting as if there would be another world war."[31] The highly respected writer and analyst emphasized the fact that although the war with Germany had ended a year ago, there had been no progress made toward a real peace conference. The Allies had promised a future peace conference in Paris, Lippmann wrote, but since the respective statesmen had failed to come to grips with the central problem of a German peace since war's end, he cautioned against undue optimism now: "If we understand why this so-called peace conference is not dealing with Germany, we shall come close to the heart of the matter."[32]

His line of reasoning was that now that the victorious Allies had displaced the power of Germany with their own, they had begun their sparring and arguing over a settlement for the former enemy state. This was but a manifestation, he continued, of an older quarrel between Churchill and Stalin that began during the war when it became apparent to the Soviet dictator that Churchill wanted to influence the course of the war not only toward a German defeat, but most importantly Western control over central and eastern Europe: "The controversy was in the last analysis political, it was whether, even though it means a longer war, the British and Americans would at the end be in physical possession of Vienna, Budapest, and the whole Balkan Peninsula. As we know, the issue was decided, with some compromise, against Mr. Churchill by President Roosevelt and our General Staff."[33]

Lippmann was convinced that the issues between Great Britain and Russia were mounting and could not be regulated. The situation was a public secret, and this was the primary reason for the current tension that the newsman found in European capitals, since, he concluded, every individual statesman "has it in the back of his mind . . . that he must act as if there were going to be a war between Britain and Russia, which will involve all the other nations."³ ⁴

Entitling his second report "The German Drama," the American columnist informed his readers that the general rejection Mr. Byrnes encountered with his treaty proposal in Europe—not just Soviet rejection—stemmed from an inadequate picture of the German situation on the part of the Secretary of State. "For the proposal, which would have been well received in 1944," Lippmann wrote, "is based on a radical misunderstanding of what is happening in Germany. It takes no account of, and indeed runs afoul of, the evolution of Soviet and British policy."³ ⁵

This meant that Byrnes' assumption deliberately ignored both the British and the Russian desire to have access to German manpower and resources if war broke out. The official American viewpoint expressed by Byrnes' efforts accepted the basic premise that the wartime allies were still united in their objective to disarm Germany. The real fact was that both of America's war partners were working on the basis that another conflict was almost inevitable, and Germany's potential made for a powerful partner in any struggle. By all odds, if war came, Germany would be the starting place. Lippmann's current assessment was: "Though battered, the Germans are still . . . the strongest nation in Europe: a duel is in progress between London and Moscow for the control of the German population, and its high military potential."³ ⁶

The reason the United States appeared to be relatively uninformed about all of this was partly a matter of geography, Lippmann reasoned. In the division of Germany, the British and the Russians received the parts of that nation that were important in terms of industrial potential and history. The Americans and the French shared the far less important southern Germany.³ ⁷ Thus, the United States was not directly involved in dealing with those features or elements that were basic to the British and Russians. Lippmann described these as ocean ports, industries, population, banks, cartels, trade unions, communication systems, centralized bureaucracy, military tradition, political apparatus, and the former capital city of Berlin.³ ⁸ Lippmann continued:

> There is also a German army, a large and good one, which surrendered to the British. The story of that surrender has still to be told in detail.

The story of what happened to that German army after surrender is still hidden behind a silken curtain. Enough is, however, known to warrant the statement that the corps of officers in this particular army were treated with exceptional consideration, with enough chivalry to justify them in feeling that their careers as professional soldiers were not necessarily and finally terminated.[39]

Lippmann characterized both British and Soviet policies in foreign affairs as simply reversions to prewar ideas that each could use Germany against the other. All of this was not easy to discern, however, for even American leadership was confused at this direction of events because the Anglo-Soviet duel, as Lippmann repeatedly described it, was largely hidden from view. Both the British and the Russians continued to agree with the United States on wartime decisions to punish the Germans and much lip service was rendered the disarmament pledge. In reality, however, both nations were pursuing policies at the lower levels that were quite contradictory, for here the contest appeared openly as one of winning the favor and support of the political and military elements of Germany. Not to be forgotten in this situation, Lippmann cautioned, were the Germans themselves, who, quick to recognize the potential in an otherwise depressing position, took their new "reeducation" with a grain of salt and looked for advantages from the two occupying rivals.[40]

Quite naturally, with the exposure that Lippmann's observations received, it was only a matter of hours before comment began. The same day that his second column appeared, President Truman was asked by reporters if he would say something about Lippmann's analysis. The American President treated it all very lightly with somewhat cynical replies, mostly to the effect that hindsight was always an easy bit of work. He did, however, refuse any real answer, insisting that since he had no firsthand knowledge of Lippmann's findings in Europe, he could offer no comment. Interestingly, the President also refused comment at the same news session on the breakdown of the Paris Conference, giving no hint that the meeting had ended in failure for Byrnes' proposal.[41]

In England, the reaction to Lippmann's material was emphatic. Admitting that 120,000 German prisoners of war were still organized into units doing mine clearance work and other special jobs, the Foreign Office described everything else Lippmann had written as sheer nonsense. The Foreign Office release pointed out that the American correspondent had not visited either Great Britain or the British zone of occupation in Germany. Particularly annoying was his reference to a "silken curtain" over British activities in their zone when, the release continued, journalists—including Russians—were given full access to the area.[42]

A rather different version was provided by another journalist on a visit to the British zone shortly after the appearance of Lippmann's articles. The journalist in question, a Mr. Hill, admitted that in touring the British zone shortly after Lippmann's columns were published, he failed to find any "phantom army." He did note, however, that "It was only at the time of my trip [June 1946] that the British, acting under the pressure of the second Russian protest [at Paris] and the Lippmann articles, began requiring German officers to remove their insignia, stop calling themselves by their rank titles, and stop saluting each other."[43]

Apparently convinced that the time was ripe for direct action at a higher level, the Soviet delegation to the Council of Foreign Ministers submitted a proposal in July which requested the immediate establishment of a special commission to enforce Allied decisions to disarm Germany and to end the current controversy once and for all on the question of the maintenance of paramilitary units. All findings were to be presented to the Allied Control Council as quickly as possible.[44] Needless to say, there was no endorsement of the Soviet proposal and no action was taken. At the same session, Molotov, in turn, gave the final rejection to Byrnes' treaty draft by dismissing the twenty-five year length as totally inadequate and countered with forty years as a minimum for control over German disarmament.[45]

The report by Britain's Foreign Minister, Ernest Bevin, on the Paris session was also revealing in that little mention was made of the Russian complaints of the past months concerning the German forces in the British zone of Germany. Instead, Bevin, after praising Byrnes' treaty proposal as offering a real basis for future peace in Europe, expressed great disappointment with the Russian behavior. In very general terms, the British Foreign Minister implied that any Soviet dissatisfaction with the current state of disarmament arrangements was no sufficient excuse for refusing Byrnes' treaty. Bevin endorsed the suggestion of a four-power commission to immediately undertake an inspection tour of "all the zones, not merely one, and see exactly what was happening."[46]

Bevin warned the Soviet Union that this was an opportunity not to be missed and not likely to come around a second time. In the same breath, he praised the United States for assuming a leadership role, and urged continued efforts undaunted by Soviet suspicions. In closing his comment on the Paris session, Bevin was firm that there would be no inspection of the British zone on the mere basis of Soviet complaint: "We cannot accept the position that the Soviet Zone is an exclusive place while our zone is wide open for inspection, and we are subject to accusations for which there is not the slightest justification."[47]

Bevin's reaction to the Byrnes proposal left much to be desired and the entire thrust of Bevin's argument appeared to be a strong effort to transfer full British support to the United States as well as the responsibility for Western world leadership. At the same time, there was a conscious move to ignore Soviet protests on British zone actions and instead to turn the tables by implying that something worth investigating on the disarmament squabble was happening in the Soviet sector. Knowing full well that there could be no general agreement on an investigative body, Bevin proposed that one be established anyway. Given the recent history of that specific proposal in the four-power council, Bevin's suggestion could be regarded as no more than empty rhetoric and no better than the tactics so often employed by the Russians.

In response to another meeting of the Foreign Ministers in early July 1946, Molotov based the reasoning for a forty year disarmament period on the fact that the two world wars had been only twenty years apart, and the disarmament of Germany had been a sad failure after the first experience.[48]

Molotov declared that anyone taking the trouble to study Byrnes' treaty draft would clearly see that the restrictions proposed for Germany were not severe enough to prevent future aggression. This then presented the question, he continued, as to just how a satisfactory treaty was to be arrived at by the big powers. His answer was that there had to be a return to the basic decisions that were developed in cooperative fashion during the war against Germany. Everyone knew, Molotov stated, that these wartime agreements contained the necessary beginnings toward an adequate disarmament of Germany, but the measures had not been carried out. In particular, Molotov continued, there had been disappointment over the negative reception given the Soviet proposal to establish an investigative body to look into the violation of these wartime agreements (Yalta and Potsdam Conferences) to disarm the Germans.[49]

If the American Secretary of State had been in the dark before and failed to achieve the diplomatic triumph he anticipated, Molotov's declaration should have provided some clarification. The question was not the correctness or incorrectness of the Soviet stand, but the apparent determination of the British to follow their own policy in Germany and have American support. The Lippmann report had not been without substance.

There is no indication that Byrnes took any serious note of either Lippmann's account or Molotov's explanations, although he was fully cognizant of the Russian complaints about the British maintaining a German army in their zone. He appeared more impressed by the British countercharges that the Russians were manufacturing war materials in their occupation area. The Secretary of State implied that when Western powers proposed a full investigation of all charges, Molotov agreed (in April 1946), but his representatives on a lower level blocked all action. Byrnes insisted that when he tried to clear the air later, Molotov said it was meaningless by then, for a policy on general disarmament for Germany had to be constructed first.[50]

There were few overt signs of concern about the breakdown in real communication as well as decreasing cooperation between the Western powers and Russia. One such sign, however, was an article in *The Economist* in December 1945,[51] that outlined the disintegration of Western-Soviet relations. It was pointed out that since the German attack on the Soviet Union in June 1941, until the Potsdam Conference, an atmosphere of cooperation among the three major allies had prevailed in relation to Germany. Now, it was noted, "the system is breaking down."[52] The "big three" were rapidly becoming two versus one.

On the level of zonal administration, the British concern for defense and administration was aggravated by the quick demobilization that occurred immediately after the war. Confronted instantly with the menace of Russia and the end of the shooting war, the requirements for a large force were still there and British military needs could not be met by voluntary enlistment. The conditions in British-occupied Germany reflected this situation.[53] In addition to the employment of German manpower for military tasks, the British Army of the Rhine also began the use of displaced persons in their zone for duty.

A body was established called the "Civil Mixed Watchmen's Service," which expanded from approximately a hundred men to over ten thousand enlistees in the period 1946 to 1947. The occupation commander was soon authorized to add a German force for similar duties numbering 45,200 men. Called the "German Service Organization" or G.S.O., the units were enlisted for three year periods and began their training with rifles and Sten guns.[54]

A newspaper carried some of the story on June 4, 1946, reporting the formation of a foreign police legion in the British zone.[55] The army issued an immediate denial of the news account, insisting that using a select number of displaced persons for guard did not constitute a "foreign police legion." There was, however, a government plan already being formulated to enlist approximately a thousand Yugoslavs, Poles, and Balts into the Civil Mixed Watchmen's Service in August, and this definitely was not public news. Later, in October of the same year, a detailed plan was drawn suggesting that each man be enlisted for three years and issued a uniform and a rifle (with fifty rounds of ammunition). The initial number of men for mid-October was 6,000. It was noted in War Office files that many of the men had been prisoners of war in Germany and feared being charged with collaboration if they returned home. Some consideration was given to merging German forces with the Service, but this was dropped for the time being.[56]

Meanwhile, both Yugoslavia and Russia protested the use of displaced persons from Yugoslavia in British service. This caused sufficient embarrassment for British authorities to consider substituting Czechs for Yugoslavs.[57] Russia complained that Great

Britain had encouraged displaced persons to work actively in the camps against the Soviet Union and presumably aid the drive for service recruitment.[58]

It is significant that by 1947, the Soviets were mentioning the United States along with Great Britain when issuing broadsides on disarmament violations involving Germany. In March 1947, at a Council of Foreign Ministers meeting, still struggling with the German demilitarization question, Molotov charged that the Western Allies seemed to have chosen to ignore Allied Control Council directives to disarm and disband the former German armed forces. The Soviet Foreign Minister insisted that there "still remain at the disposal of Commanders of the British and American occupation forces undisbanded German military units and services which formerly belonged to Germany's land forces, air fleet and navy. These so-called 'auxiliary units' retain their military organization and are commanded by German officers who enjoy rights of disciplinary action, which facilitates the preservation of German army cadres."[59] Citing what he termed "official reports," Molotov stated that as of January 1947, the British maintained a German force of 81,358 men and the Americans some 9,000 men.[60]

During the summer of 1947, it was reported that the British authorities had dissolved the last remnants of the immediate postwar German military formations and began the establishment of a volunteer body called the German Civil Labour Organization, containing many enlistees from the eastern portion of Germany. The organization quickly numbered over 70,000 men.[61]

All of these events are the more interesting because of the fact that in December 1946, by an agreement signed in New York, there had been a fusion of the British and American zones. The major reason for this action, reflecting the difficult economic position of Great Britain, was to improve the fiscal situation in Germany. This meant establishing a bipartite administration as well as transferring significant duties of government on the lower levels to the Germans. Quite clearly, it also signaled the failure of any possibility of a quadripartite agreement and this had been emphasized by the impasse that emerged from the Foreign Ministers' Conference in Moscow.[62] It may be concluded that this action served strong notice that British and American goals for a

German future had virtually merged into one. Thus, it would appear all the more surprising that United States' knowledge of British zonal activities remained relatively limited. Part of the explanation rested, no doubt, with the clearer identity of United States' interests with those of Great Britain in the burgeoning Cold War atmosphere and, indeed, the assumption of leadership in that struggle by the Americans.

It is interesting that the subject of German war prisoners still in Allied hands by mid-1947, rarely became an object of discussion in all of the international debates on German disarmament. Since all parties, including Russia, had used, and continued to use, German war prisoners in large number for their own purposes, there appeared to be an unspoken understanding that it was not an issue. However, from time to time, newspapers picked up stories on the subject. One such appeared in The Manchester *Guardian* in July 1947, urging quick repatriation for the German prisoners still remaining in Allied hands. The article provided figures on the number of German prisoners of war still held: Russia, 890,000; France, 600,000; Great Britain, 280,000; the Middle East, 80,000; Yugoslavia, 70,000; Belgium, 40,000; Poland, 30,000; Holland, 10,000; Czechoslovakia, 8,000; and Luxemburg, 4,000, for a grand total of 2,012,000 men.[63] The *Guardian* expressed strong doubts that the "official" figure for Russia reflected the true number in Soviet hands and hinted at at least double the figure. Britain was blamed for not following the American example of releasing all German prisoners of war quickly. The program then being pursued returned only 15,000 Germans a month to civilian society, and this meant at least another year before all had been released. "In the meantime," the article concluded, "German prisoners must filter slowly back under arbitrary and individual plans, full of resentment from France and Britain, broken in health and spirit from Russia."[64] Perhaps the fact that German prisoners were located in individual states rather than Germany proper acted to delay concern and attention.

Despite a House of Commons committee report in October 1947, to the effect that "disarmament [of Germany] is virtually complete,"[65] the Soviet member of the Allied Control Council, Marshal Sokolovsky, released a strong criticism of Western policies. As the Soviet Marshal prepared to leave Germany for a

London meeting of the Council of Foreign Ministers, he declared that the Western Allies and especially Great Britain, had failed to effectively disarm the Germans. For the benefit of the *Taegliche Rundschau* (a Soviet military government newspaper), Sokolovsky stated that "remnants of German military formations are being retained in the British zone under the guise of so-called labour corps," and added that they had also left the naval installations at Kiel intact.[66]

Sokolovsky's statement was too important to pass unnoticed, and as the convening of the Foreign Ministers Council was being reported, his words were given press attention. *The Times* carried news of the situation on November 24, speculating that there would probably be no formal reply to the Marshal's charges.[67] *The Times* reported the gist of Sokolovsky's statement in Berlin to the Control Council, commenting that similar complaints had been forthcoming from the Russians for months, admitting, however, that this differed to the extent that it was delivered before the council and just after the Marshal had returned from Moscow.[68]

Quoting the American General Clay, *The Times* stated that the comments of Sokolovsky would probably be ignored. Clay implied that he was not going to make an issue of it, and characterized the Russian's statement as a "misunderstanding." The American General said that an explanation should have been sought by Sokolovsky before making any charges.[69]

The Times, however, suggested that such a thing could not be so easily dismissed as Clay seemed to think. Germans in the Soviet zone as well as in the Western zones were very apprehensive about the situation and expected the London negotiations to break down. Elaborating on Sokolovsky's Berlin statement, *The Times* reported that the Marshal accused the British of virtually no progress on disarmament in Germany for the past six months "and trying to save German naval bases from demilitarization."[70]

In such an atmosphere of constant mutual recriminations any desire for recapturing the earlier period of cooperation vanished and the Cold War gained momentum. The speed was increased in March 1948, when Sokolovsky stalked out of the Allied Control Council, preparing the way for a Soviet blockade of Berlin, and the Western Allies concluded a military alliance in Brussels. Calling for a command structure under Field Marshal Montgomery, Great

Britain, France, Belgium, the Netherlands and Luxemburg began the preparation for a "Uniforce" that would help protect them against Soviet attack. It was the first time in British history that such a military alliance with continental powers was made in peacetime.[71]

By now all pretense was gone that wartime visions could somehow be salvaged, and even the most optimistic had to admit that Western-Soviet cooperation was fast becoming nonexistent. Germany's future position was now an even more vital question, and obviously a "reappraisal" by the occupying powers was necessary. In reporting on the Brussels Pact, *The Times* wondered whether the Western Allies had recognized the role that Western Germany might play in defending Europe, while *Pravda* replied that the treaty was an openly aggressive move.[72] The Soviets did not limit themselves to rhetoric, for restrictions on Western access to Berlin were already in effect, and in June 1948, a full-scale blockade of that city began.

In a House of Commons speech at the end of June, Foreign Minister Bevin reviewed some of these events. He reminded his audience that just a few short years before, British troops had marched eastward to Wismar on the Baltic, but in accordance with previous agreement, surrendered territory to the Russians. Churchill, still representing his Woodford constituency, was quick to remind the Foreign Minister that British forces had "retired" as far as 150 miles in some places to accommodate the Russians.[73]

Angrily citing chapter and verse of mutual arrangements arrived at with the Russians since war's end concerning Allied access to Berlin, Bevin asked how it was now possible for them to do this. Besides specific access agreements—written and unwritten—already in force there were Western commitments to provision over half of the city of Berlin with coal, food and other supplies. How was this to be done? The Potsdam Agreement was based on the assumption that economic and political unity for Germany was the desired future goal, Bevin continued, and it was now quite obvious that the Soviets never honored that fact.[74]

Speculating on Soviet motives, the British Foreign Minister refused to accept the technical excuses offered by the Russians. Concluding that the intent was to throw chaos into the Western camp, Bevin stated: "His Majesty's Government cannot submit to that. . . . We cannot abandon those stout-hearted Berlin democrats who are refusing to bow to Soviet pressure."[75] Shortly thereafter, the Soviets announced their withdrawal from the Berlin *Kommandatura.* What incredible changes in a brief three years!

The wartime Allies had now managed in a short thirty-six months to bring themselves to the brink of another war, and this time against each other. No amount of calm talk could conceal a situation so explosive that a downed airplane or a shot in haste could mean war. In this deepening crisis, the prospects of creating a new German army—east and west—suddenly assumed meaning. An American general wrote of the tense time: "Only three years after her defeat, we started to resurrect the Germany we had sworn to destroy. We needed this Germany as our partner in the defense of Europe against our former ally, the Soviet Union."[76]

Of course, it did not require great insight or special knowledge to recognize the direction of Western-Soviet relations in the summer of 1948. West German rearmament was already being firmly predicted in German newspapers, and other European news bulletins remarked on the beginning of a new period for Germany.[77] The German press reaction to the possibility of contributing to some Western defense structure was somewhat mixed, however. It was clear that danger was imminent, but the past three years had left frustration and bitterness too, which was directed at the victors. Now the dilemma was "a case of damned if you do and damned if you don't."[78]

The mass of German people had little knowledge of British efforts to retain intact a German force after the war. Now, however, a new charge surfaced that the Western Allies were raising a German army in secret. This was echoed in publications around Germany primarily as the result of a press conference held by anti-Nazi leader and German publisher Eugen Kogon. In November 1948, upon return to Germany from the European Federalist Congress in Rome, Mr. Kogon was reported as saying that the Western Allies were already in the process of establishing a West German army. He stated that this was being done completely without the knowledge or support of German politicians or the German public. The fact that Western interest in a German rearmament had become public fare greatly overshadowed the controversy surrounding Kogon's exact statement. German editorials soon began to confront the fundamental issues involved in a nation divided, without sovereignty, dependent on its survival to foreign states, and now caught up in a life-death contest between the wartime victors. The crux of much of the argument centered on German contributions to Western defense without real sovereignty. Although the point was made that if the alleged German army was actually in existence as some said, and had been for some time, then the argument for sovereignty had already lost meaning.[79]

Another interpretation was attempted by one German newspaper with the suggestion, in light of a French news account reporting that if war with Russia came, the best position for Western defense was between the Rhine and the Elbe, that those Germans now being trained for military use were really mercenaries.[80] Some newsmen told of interviewing American Congressmen in Berlin in December 1948, and indicated with the airlift now well into the winter months, that the United States was seriously discussing arming the Germans. Congressman Paul W. Shafer of Michigan, when asked about the rumor that former Wehrmacht general Halder was exploring his contacts in preparation for a new German army, said, "Why, certainly. No problem at all. They've got the raw material down there [Western Zones] all right."[81]

The wartime concerns of the Allied powers that had focused so strongly on a postwar Germany that would be disarmed and patrolled for a generation to come had disappeared. In fact, the exact reversal had become the reality of the day and the concerns in 1948 were those of assessing Germany's war potential for possible use in case the Cold War became hot. The cry was not disarmament and control, but rearmament and cooperation. In 1946 Byrnes and Molotov sparred and quibbled over a proposed treaty wording that would guarantee German disarmament for twenty-five or forty years; in 1948, the question on both sides was how quickly can the Germans be rearmed? Future students of twentieth-century history, examining these events from the perspective of a hundred years or so, may only express confusion and bewilderment if they confine their studies to official documentation.

NOTES

1. D. N. Pritt, *The Labour Government, 1945-1951* (New York: International Publishers, 1963), p. 53.

2. J. Byrnes, *Speaking Frankly*, pp. 171-72.

3. Loc. cit.

4. Ibid., p. 174.

5. *The Times* (London), February 6, 1946.

6. Ibid., February 22, 1946.

7. Ibid., February 26, 1946.

8. Loc. cit.

9. *The Times* (London), February 6, 1946.

10. Ibid., February 26, 1946.

11. Loc. cit.

12. U.S., Dept. of State, *Occupation of Germany: Policy and Progress, 1945-46*, pp. 101-02.

13. Austrian nationals were exceptions to the rule for they were subject to the decisions of the Allied Control Council for Austria.

14. Great Britain had some 500,000 Germans in Commonwealth states in 1946, and 74,000 POWs in England. France had about 470,000 Germans employed in December 1945.

15. See F. Kopp, *Chronik der Wiederbewaffnung in Deutschland*, pp. 30-31.

16. Loc. cit.

17. W. H. McNeill, *America, Britain and Russia* (New York: Oxford University Press, 1953), p. 659.

18. D. N. Pritt, *The Labour Government*, p. 13. Churchill had, in fact, proposed in May 1945, that the Labour-Liberal coalition continue until the end of the Japanese war with no national elections. Attlee suggested an election for October; however, Churchill rejected this and thus the July date was selected. See A.J.P. Taylor, *English History, 1914-1945* (New York: Oxford University Press, 1965), p. 595.

19. Pritt, *Labour Government*, p. 63.

20. *Vital Speeches of the Day*, XII (March 15, 1946), p. 331.

21. Loc. cit.

22. Ibid., p. 332.

23. Pritt, *Labour Government*, pp. 65-66.

24. New York *Times*, March 14, 1946.

25. McNeill, *America, Britain and Russia*, p. 660. The author also suggested that while British opinion stiffened toward the Russians earlier than it did in the U.S., it did not run quite so deep: "Long experience of international affairs in some measure armed the British public against excessive optimism and equally against excessive moral indignation when hopes were disappointed." Loc. cit.

26. *Vital Speeches*, XII (March 15, 1946), p. 331.

27. C. Barnett, *Britain and Her Army, 1509-1970* (New York: Morrow, 1970), p. 485.

28. B.R. von Oppen, *Documents on Germany under Occupation*, p. 138.

29. Ibid., p. 139.

30. Los Angeles *Times*, May 7 and 9, 1946.

31. Ibid., May 7, 1946.

32. Loc. cit.

33. Loc. cit.
34. Loc. cit.
35. Los Angeles *Times*, May 9, 1946.
36. Loc. cit.
37. As someone commented at the time, Great Britain got Germany's industrial belt and America got the scenery.
38. Los Angeles *Times*, May 9, 1946.
39. Loc. cit.
40. Loc. cit.
41. New York *Times*, May 10, 1946.
42. Ibid., May 13, 1946.
43. R. Hill, *Struggle for Germany*, p. 222.
44. *F.R.U.S., 1946*, Vol. II, pp. 878-79.
45. V. M. Molotov, *Problems of Foreign Policy: Speeches and Statements April 1945-November 1948* (Moscow: Foreign Language Publishing House, 1949), p. 55.
46. Von Oppen, *Documents on Germany under Occupation*, p. 140.
47. Ibid., p. 141.
48. Molotov, *Problems of Foreign Policy*, p. 59.
49. Ibid., pp. 60-61.
50. J. Byrnes, *Speaking Frankly*, p. 177.
51. "The Russian case," December 8, 1945.
52. Ibid., p. 819.
53. C. Barnett, *Britain and Her Army*, p. 487.
54. G.B., W.O., 32/11783/Docs. 1A-11A.
55. *The Times* (London).
56. W.O., 32/11783, Docs. 1A-11A.
57. Ibid., Docs. 40A, 84A and 87A.
58. E. F. Penrose, "Negotiating on Refugees and Displaced Persons, 1946," in R. Dennett and J. E. Johnson, eds., *Negotiating with the Russians* (Boston: World Peace Foundation, 1951), p. 158.
59. Molotov, *Problems of Foreign Policy*, p. 346.
60. Loc. cit.
61. F. Kopp, *Chronik*, p. 34.
62. Von Oppen, *Docs. on Germany*, p. 251.
63. The Manchester *Guardian*, July 26, 1947.
64. Loc. cit. See E. Maschke, ed., *Zur Geschichte der deutschen Kriegsgefangenen des Zweiten Weltkrieges*, 22 vols. (Muenchen: Verlag Ernst und Werner Gieseking, 1967).
65. Von Oppen, *Docs. on Germany*, p. 252.
66. Keesing's Research Report, *Germany and Eastern Europe since 1945* (New York: Scribner's, 1973), pp. 25-26.
67. *The Times* (London), November 24, 1947.
68. Loc. cit.
69. Loc. cit.
70. Loc. cit.
71. C. Barnett, *Britain and Her Army*, pp. 482-83.
72. Quoted in E. Willenz, "Early discussions regarding a defense contribution in Germany, 1948-1950," U.S. Air Force Project, Rand Research Memorandum 968, *German Studies* (Santa Monica, Calif.: RAND, 1952), p. 21.
73. Von Oppen, *Docs. on Germany*, pp. 309-10.
74. Ibid., p. 311.
75. Ibid., p. 313.

76. A. C. Wedemeyer, *Wedemeyer Reports* (New York: Henry Holt, 1958), p. 92.

77. E. Willenz, "Early discussions regarding a defense contribution in Germany," Rand RM-968, p. 2.

78. Ibid., p. 3.

79. Ibid., pp. 4-7.

80. Ibid., pp. 7-8. The German newspaper quoted was the *Rheinsche Post*, November 27, 1948; it carried the reference to the French paper *Figaro*.

81. W. G. Burchett, *Cold War in Germany* (Melbourne, Australia: World Unity Publications, 1950), p. 166.

Chapter 7

FROM ALLIES TO ENEMIES

It is doubtful if the first postwar generation of people living in the Western world will ever be fully persuaded that the burden of responsibility for Cold War origins rests primarily with Great Britain. The identification of United States policies with those of the British became so all-pervasive by 1947-48 that the earlier period of differences, clouded by wartime expediencies, became blurred in popular thinking. There is evidence of very sharp differences between the United States and Britain in their opinion and policy vis-à-vis the Soviet Union and, secondarily, the manner in which postwar German disarmament was approached. Quite clearly, the complexity of the subject as well as overlapping influences preclude a tight compartmentalization; however, this does not make an examination of differences impossible.

On a very broad scale there is no question that generally British leadership regarded U.S. friendship toward the Soviet Union during the war years as naive and very dangerous for the future. One writer expressed it like this: "By 1945, the British leaders had strong misgivings, only the Americans seemed blissfully unaware of the realities of the postwar world, making large concessions to the Russians and assuming an equal amount of good will on the other side. Their awakening was rude and they reacted the more violently, after having realized that they had been duped."[1] A gross generalization, but not an unfamiliar theme in many British circles. As the popularity of Cold War history grew by leaps and bounds, journalist, researcher and historian hammered away at American innocence—indeed, stupidity—in not recognizing the Russian menace early on in the war.[2]

It was not too difficult, in retrospect, of course, to pinpoint any number of specific instances to buttress the British charges. It became almost "common knowledge" that of the major western leaders, Churchill alone faced "reality." His anti-Bolshevik stance had long been history and the record was replete with his warnings. Perhaps, as one historian has written, Churchill counted too much on U.S. friendship, and therefore "had to invent the Bolshevik peril, whether it existed or not. Common danger from Soviet Russia was needed to keep them together once Germany was defeated."[3]

From its very inception, the Bolshevik force had been dealt with by Western powers at long distance. From 1917 to 1945, "confrontations" did not exist in the postwar sense; it was only with the end of World War II in Europe that both sides found it necessary to sit down together and attempt cooperative solutions to mutual problems: "Germany was the vacuum where both ideology and power converged from both sides, and collided."[4]

There is no denying that in such an atmosphere there were few credentials in the Western camp better than those of Winston Churchill, and his already great reputation was enhanced by his longevity in leadership. President Truman was not even a national statesman, let alone international, and was far more susceptible to Churchill's cautions than F.D.R. had been: "Now and not before, Churchill was free to sound the anti-Bolshevik alarm and had to do so. It was the only way of securing American assistance for Great Britain."[5]

Britain's wartime Prime Minister had sought in vain to persuade Roosevelt of the importance of establishing a position of power toward the Soviet Union during the final months of war. His efforts did not go unnoticed by those American officials who dealt with him, however. Churchill's arguments that a strong Germany was an essential in the bulwark against Russia was becoming increasingly strident by April of 1945, although in some quarters of Washington, there was great skepticism concerning its validity.[6]

The supreme importance of the Russo-German war had, of course, been fully recognized in the decisive year of 1943. What had seemed like a dream come true in 1941 now began to assume the proportions of a possible nightmare less than two years later. Of utmost concern to Western allied planners in early summer of 1943 was the time factor, for they knew that the Germans would win or lose on the basis of their performance in Russia before autumn arrived.[7] However, granting the fact that Churchill's expressed apprehensions were consistent, there were also American fears voiced at the time. The record has tended somewhat to obscure this fact because, unlike Churchill, the American warnings did not remain constant. Instead, after 1943, when the immediate anxieties of a separate peace subsided and Stalin became committed to unconditional surrender, American criticism of possible Soviet intentions subsided too. Again, toward the end of the war critical voices were raised once more, but not sufficiently strong to represent an arm of American policy.[8] There was a noticeable shift in American attitude toward Russia that began as the war closed, however, and it was soon to constitute policy. It did not mean that the United States had fully adopted Britain's policies though: "The war ended with the United States and the United Kingdom—close partners that they were—almost as far apart on European problems as the West was from the East."[9]

The exigencies of war had masked a good deal of mutual dissatisfaction with each other's attitudes and behavior on a number of issues from separate peace to German occupation zones. These differences did not escape Soviet eyes and greatly fueled their hostility toward Great Britain as the war drew to its conclusion.[10] There was little doubt that American opinion historically considered the Nazis a greater danger to Europe's future than the Soviets, but the same generalization was not applicable to Great Britain.[11]

The possibility of a separate peace in the west with Germany— as well as a possible Russo-German peace in the east[12] —still remains a murky subject, but British interest was not a dead issue in 1943-44. Quite obviously the war situation had greatly altered from 1941 to 1943, and despite a British promise in July 1941 never to make a separate peace with the Germans (as well as a 1942 Treaty of Alliance with the Soviet Union),[13] matters did look very different after Stalingrad. Admittedly, the evidence is not at all strong that British leaders gave serious thought to a separate German peace in midwar; however, unlike in the United States, the subject did circulate among the top echelon persons and rumors have persisted.[14]

The separate peace threat was not ignored by the United States; quite to the contrary, for the push to gain unanimous allied approval for an unconditional surrender doctrine had been chiefly American. Leaving aside the postwar controversy over the exact origin and intent of the unconditional surrender declaration, the fact remains that as it began to prove increasingly burdensome to the Allies, America was quickly given the dubious credit for its inception. It was not only the anxiety of a Russo-German peace that disturbed Roosevelt, but the desire to placate Stalin for the postponement of a second front long promised.[15] Official U.S. policy continued to support unconditional surrender to the very end, although there was concern that the other allies might avoid it somehow. The American Secretary of State Stettinius noted in an April 1945 message that the policy "has never been altered nor modified in any way, and should not now be permitted to be compromised during the final stages of military operations against Germany."[16]

In January of the same year, Churchill had already began to hint at other than an unconditional surrender outcome of the German war. Speaking before the House of Commons on the subject, the British Prime Minister admitted that he had endorsed Roosevelt's Casablanca proclamation at the time because matters still "hung in the balance." Now, it was different, he said, victory was within grasp and it was appropriate to take into consideration the altered scene. Carefully and with unmistakable clarity, the Prime Minister suggested that serious thought should be given as to whether or not one wanted to really destroy the Germans. By skillful use of language, he was able to convey the idea that while he was just as much in favor of unconditional surrender as ever, should one not be aware of the times and temper justice with mercy?[17]

Later, Lord Hankey, a cabinet minister in Churchill's wartime administration, revealed some of the British thinking that was current at the time of the Prime Minister's statement: "The only nation that gained any advantage from the policy of Unconditional Surrender was Russia, who, owing to the lengthening of the war, was able to overrun Eastern Europe and there to impose her own political system."[18]

With the benefit of hindsight, several of Britain's wartime leaders were later able to add other dimensions to their complaints about U.S. policy. The insistence upon "unconditional surrender" was blamed by Montgomery for the postwar problems in Germany, and he labeled the policy "a very great mistake—and was now to be proved so."[19] This was the same theme belabored by Ernest Bevin in 1949, when he was Secretary of State for Foreign Affairs. After defending British policy in occupied Germany, Bevin reviewed the Casablanca declaration as an act upon which "neither the British Cabinet nor any other Cabinet had a chance to say a word. It was in the middle of a war, and it was just made. . . . it left us with a Germany without law, without a constitution, without a single person with whom we could deal. . . . I cannot pay too great a tribute to the military commanders and political advisers who were left with a shambles out of which they had to create a new Germany."[20]

Churchill agreed with Bevin's statement, noting that he, Churchill, had had little choice in not giving voice support to Roosevelt since the American President made the announcement without prior consultation. The main thing now, however, was to stop dismantling factories in Germany that could be useful to Western defense and to win full German support in the process.[21]

One line of argument that followed from the insistence on German unconditional surrender—although Churchill did not think "unconditional surrender had played an important part in the conditions in which the war was brought to an end"[22]—was the belief that it forced German partition. The idea here being that if there had been any scrap of government whatsoever allowed to continue in Germany, the Allies would have worked through that structure to rule and unity would have been preserved.[23]

Of course, there was some dissatisfaction expressed by the Americans with the way Germany was ultimately divided at war's end. Some of this was predetermined by the invasion pattern and could not be avoided since the American forces were on the "right" at Normandy and remained there as they wheeled into

Germany. "It has frequently been said," one description goes, "that, whereas Poland and Russia got the bread basket and Britain the heart of German industry, the United States got the scenery."[24] An important factor here was the British control of much of the remainder of German industry in the Ruhr and Rhine areas as well as its future potential. British opinion at the statesman's level was already critical of the view discussed at Potsdam that intended sharp limitations of German industry. The issue was widely discussed in Great Britain, but generally ignored by the United States.[25] The British did not allow the wholesale destruction of war materials in their area of control and prided themselves, in fact, on their "realistic" policy as opposed to Washington's "illusions."[26]

The general argument had already surfaced a number of times and manifested itself in different issues, however, they were usually quite directly related. During the closing months of the war and far removed from the conference table, the opposing aims of Great Britain and the United States were seen in the conflict that developed between Generals Montgomery and Eisenhower. There had been clashes behind the scenes before this, but the differences between the two men had remained relatively minor in nature. Now, with mounting concern on Churchill's part and with an almost fanatic zeal that he simply had to awaken the United States to the Soviet peril or take unilateral action, the very real problem of how much of Germany could and should be conquered arose. The question of what should be occupied was really no problem; the crux of the dilemma, as Churchill viewed it, rested upon how sizable a portion could be seized before the Russians moved in. He attached tremendous importance to ending the war in a bargaining position, and this meant pushing as far east as possible before the final shot sounded.

There was no doubt in Churchill's mind that the greater territory held by the West, the stronger their hand at the peace table, and he was not about to heed a "standstill order."[27] The fact that Churchill's policy to push as far as possible despite U.S. disapproval was later to be highly praised meant, conversely, that much criticism was directed at Eisenhower, especially over Berlin. Churchill's successor, Clement Attlee, was adamant in his view that the United States had not properly understood the situation

in Europe and that Eisenhower had allowed the Russians to
penetrate too far westward. His gloomy conclusion was that such
circumstances forced Great Britain to cooperate on many things
that were absolutely wrong.[28]

It may not be an exaggeration to describe Montgomery's efforts
to beat the Russians into the Baltic at the end of April 1945, as "a
battle designed not only to beat the German enemy, but also a
new enemy from the East—the erstwhile Russian ally!"[29] Montgomery's own words provided some support for this interpretation, for he rarely failed to offer the opinion later that the United
States and Great Britain could have had their way in Europe if
only Vienna, Prague and Berlin had been captured, for then "the
position would have been different. We now had to begin to pay
the price for that failure."[30] It was obvious that he did not really
mean "we" so much as the "failure" of the United States and
most specifically, Eisenhower. Later, Nikita Khrushchev observed
that although both Montgomery and Eisenhower were products of
a bourgeois society, they lived by different codes of behavior.[31]

Some points of difference between the two Allied generals
remain clear. On the matter of preventing Russia's westward push
by occupying all possible territory in her wake before the war was
over, the two men were absolutely opposed. Montgomery described those last days as a period of acute awareness on his part
of the menace the Russians were becoming, for they were now
more of a threat than the Germans: "As we moved eastwards," he
wrote, "the Prime Minister and Eisenhower both became anxious
lest I might not be able to 'head off' the Russians from getting to
Schleswig-Holstein, and then occupying Denmark. Both sent me
messages about it."[32] But neither the Eisenhower papers[33] nor
his book *Crusade in Europe*[34] make the slightest reference to
securing northern Germany and Denmark before the Russians
arrived, and no mention is made of a telegram to Montgomery on
the subject.

The conflict is well illustrated again in the entire surrender
process on the Western front. Montgomery, reflecting no doubt
much of Churchill's thinking, was determined to circumvent the
unconditional surrender policy by gathering in as many German
troops as he was capable of doing, and this meant a sizeable
percentage of the defeated Wehrmacht. Despite the popular

conception that unconditional surrender prevailed, the fact remains that it did not, for Montgomery ignored the agreed-upon policy, and as one chronicler of the year 1945 noted: "There was considerable criticism in American quarters of this separate surrender, but this has never worried Montgomery."[35] The British General was fully prepared to render lip service to the unconditional surrender formula, but in reality he adjusted his interpretation of that policy to fit his own views and accepted all German soldiers who came forward to surrender.[36]

In a message dated May 4, 1945, General Eisenhower reinterated his view of the German surrender by stating that "I consider that it would be highly desirable for the surrender on the Russian front and the surrender on this front to be exactly timed so that hostilities will cease simultaneously."[37]

Hitler's successor, Grand Admiral Karl Doenitz, has steadfastly supported the separate surrender that Montgomery made possible for him. Still defending his accomplishment of rescuing millions of Germans for the West, the retired Admiral wrote in 1971: "The discussion with the English forces concerning a partial surrender took place on May 3, 1945, between Montgomery and Admiral von Friedeburg, who had been sent by me for this purpose."[38] Doenitz had already said as much in his *Memoirs* by stating that Montgomery had been amenable to the idea of a separate peace all along and signed just such an agreement on May 4th. He also stated that he knew very well that Eisenhower was strongly opposed to it, for he already has contacted the Supreme Allied Commander and received a refusal.[39]

To this date, the old Admiral continues to view his evacuation of Germans westward as a major wartime achievement. He claims to have begun the process as early as late 1944. He said that he received an official count on May 9, 1945, indicating that from January 23, 1945, to May 8, 1945, he had successfully moved 2,022,602 German people through the harbors of the western Baltic and away from possible Russian capture. His opinion is that this figure was vastly underestimated, and he suggests that future research will raise it considerably.[40]

When asked about the conditions in those final days that permitted such a flow of Germans westward, Doenitz replied: "It went on uninterrupted thanks to the generous interpretation of this partial surrender by the English, because actually the surrender of German shipping was supposed to occur on May 5, 1945. To this day [April 29, 1975], I remain grateful to Montgomery."[41]

Perhaps Montgomery felt he had managed to circumvent the letter of Eisenhower's determination to achieve a simultaneous surrender on all Allied fronts, but had preserved the spirit. If so, he was mistaken, for there was no way possible to conceal the remnants of the huge German army over which he had assumed control.

Of course, if the United States and Great Britain had been of one mind on Russia in April 1945, it would have been possible to have insisted upon Stalin's strict adherence to every questionable aspect of the Yalta agreements, and later Potsdam too. However, it would have meant in addition to an altered stance in U.S. policy toward Russia, a readiness to go to war with a current ally if necessary. While the thought appeared horrifying to some, it was thought nevertheless.[42]

It is clear that Churchill tried to bring the United States around to his view as the war entered its final stage and failing that, did everything he could to prepare Great Britain for the eventuality of a lone confrontation with Russia. What is not clear is just how far Churchill was prepared to go. In light of the extensive Russian condemnation of his actions accusing the wartime Prime Minister of deliberately seeking war with a former ally, there were those who defended his actions, insisting that Churchill did not wish war.[43] On the other hand, who is to say exactly what was in the British leader's mind? It is legitimate to suggest that while Churchill may not have wished for war with the Soviet Union, his actions and utterances certainly indicated a willingness to open a conflict if he deemed it necessary. It should not be forgotten that ultimately he probably would have received the support of the United States, and he knew it.

Postwar developments strongly supported Churchill's early warnings and thereby greatly enhanced his already monumental reputation as a statesman. However, 1946 was the postwar period and things were quite different from the way they were in 1945; American disenchantment with the Soviet Union was well under way.

Beginning with the Woodford talk on November 23, 1954, and until the last official pronouncements on December 14, a curtain was momentarily opened to reveal some facets of Churchill's behavior at a critical moment in world history. In many ways, the revealing glimpse raised more questions than it answered. The parliamentary debates showed efforts by Churchill to prevent any pursuance of the matter and that he hoped to bury it entirely with the problematical explanation that his message had been burned. It is also extremely curious that after the Prime Minister's initial concession of having been confused, there seemed to be no second doubts in his mind that there had been a telegram and that he had very definitely dispatched it.

At one point in the House debates when there was prolonged questioning of the Prime Minister on the exact routine employed in handling documents of a secret classification, Churchill conceded that while messages might be destroyed in the field in wartime, copies were kept at home. In the course of questioning, it was also brought out that Churchill had moved quickly after the Woodford incident to contact Montgomery in America to ascertain if the telegram was in his possession.[44]

While there is no evidence that General Eisenhower knew of the message in question, it would appear that the Allied commander was not surprised at its existence. In a letter to General Marshall near the end of the war, Eisenhower vented some of his anger toward Montgomery for being such an irritant, and "attacked Churchill for his direct dealings with Montgomery—his meddlesomeness and his continued interference outside of channels."[45]

The strength of position and vindication that Churchill felt in 1954 was plain in the stance he assumed when attacked for the Woodford speech. Telegram or not, he knew more than anyone else that the world had turned 180 degrees from May of 1945, and that there would be broad and strong support for what he had said. As the Prime Minister reiterated what his feelings had been in May 1945, and there were cries of "Shame!" in the House of Commons, he persisted, "I am telling you the story quite bluntly and plainly."[46]

Unquestionably, to the man in the street (unless he was German), the very idea of the Western Allies utilizing a defeated German army to embark upon a new conflict with Soviet Russia was preposterous. Several years later such a possibility did not look nearly so remote. Meanwhile, the Cold War "story" had become familiar reading for a postwar world.

Innumerable writings detail the origin and history of the Cold War struggle. Actually, origin and history should read "origins and histories" to correctly reflect the enormous amount of controversy that exists in terms of documenting the beginnings and tracing the developments that led to the divided world of the fifties and sixties.

NOTES

1. W. Laqueur, *Russia and Germany: A Century of Conflict* (Boston: Little, Brown, 1965), p. 272.

2. Ibid., p. 273. See also G. Alperovitz, "How did the Cold War begin?" *New York Review of Books*, VII (March 23, 1967), pp. 6-12; P. Seabury, *The Rise and Decline of the Cold War* (New York: Basic Books, 1967), pp. 46-47; and M. Balfour, "Another look at 'Unconditional Surrender,' " *International Affairs*, Vol. 46, No. 4 (October 1970), pp. 719-37.

3. A.J.P. Taylor, *English History* (New York: Oxford University Press, 1965), p. 586.

4. P. Seabury, *Rise and Decline of the Cold War*, p. 58.

5. Taylor, op. cit., p. 593.

6. *Morgenthau Diary*, pp. 1179-1180.

7. *F.R.U.S., The Conferences at Washington and Quebec, 1943*, p. 274.

8. See J. L. Gaddis, *The United States and the Origins of the Cold War*, p. 199; M. Clark, *Calculated Risk* (New York: Harpers, 1950), p. 493; E. H. Cookridge, *Gehlen: Spy of the Century* (London: Transworld Publishers, 1972), pp. 167-68; and M. Blumenson, *The Patton Papers, 1940-1945* (Boston: Houghton Mifflin, 1972), Vol. 2, p. 698.

9. M. Matloff, "The Soviet Union and the War in the West," in A. Eisenstadt, ed., *American History: Recent Interpretations*, p. 432. See also Alperovitz, *Atomic Diplomacy*, pp. 68-71.

10. E. Meehan, *The British Left Wing and Foreign Policy* (New Jersey: Rutgers University Press, 1960), p. 69.

11. M. Balfour, "Another look at 'Unconditional Surrender,' " *International Affairs*, Vol. 46, No. 4 (October 1970), p. 728.

12. See H. W. Koch, "The spectre of a Separate Peace in the East: Russo-German 'Peace Feelers,' 1942-44," *Journal of Contemporary History*, 10:3 (July 1975), pp. 531-49.

13. Ibid., p. 730; and Eduard Tàborský, "Beneš and Stalin—Moscow, 1943 and 1945," *Journal of Central European Affairs*, XIII (July 1953), p. 155.

14. See A. Werth, *The Year of Stalingrad*, p. 273; Viscount Templewood, *Complacent Dictator* (New York: Alfred A. Knopf, 1947), pp. 308-10; R. Umiastowski, *Poland, Russia and Great Britain, 1941-1945* (London: Hollis and Carter, 1945), p. 425;

B. Crozier, *Franco* (Boston: Little, Brown, 1967), p. 374; F. O. Miksche, *Unconditional Surrender: The Roots of World War III* (London: Faber and Faber, 1952), p. 38; and D. Dilks, ed., *The Diaries of Sir Alexander Cadogan, 1938-1945* (New York: G. P. Putnam, 1972), p. 590.

15. J. L. Chase, "Unconditional surrender reconsidered," *Political Science Quarterly*, LXX, No. 2 (June 1955), p. 277; and J. L. Gaddis, *U.S. and Origins of Cold War*, p. 9.

16. F.R.U.S., 1945, Vol. III, p. 752.

17. *House of Commons Debates*, printed in von Oppen, *Documents on Germany under Occupation*, pp. 3-4.

18. "Unconditional Surrender," *The Contemporary Review*, v. 176 (October 1949), pp. 197-98.

19. *Memoirs*, p. 319.

20. *House of Commons Debates*, printed in von Oppen, *Documents on Germany under Occupation*, pp. 408-09.

21. Ibid., pp. 411-12. Actually, later the same year, November 1949, Churchill recalled for Bevin some correspondence in 1942 in which the U.S. and British intent to demand unconditional surrender was mentioned and had been received by Bevin. He was then Deputy Prime Minister and his answer in the correspondence revealed that he was fully in agreement. Ibid., pp. 437-39.

22. Ibid., p. 438.

23. M. Balfour, "Another look at "Unconditional Surrender,' " *International Affairs*, p. 720.

24. J. Warburg, *Germany–Bridge or Battleground?*, p. 20.

25. Ibid., p. 40.

26. B. Gardner, *The Year that Changed the World, 1945*, p. 167.

27. J. Wheeler-Bennett and A. Nichols, *Semblance of Peace*, p. 276.

28. F. Williams, *A Prime Minister Remembers*, pp. 51-52.

29. C. Whiting, *End of the War*, p. 1.

30. *Memoirs*, p. 340. Montgomery wrote: "I had always put Berlin as a priority objective; . . . Eisenhower had agreed with me about the great importance of the German capitol, and has said, 'Clearly, Berlin is the main prize.' . . . but now [March 31, 1945], he did not agree." Ibid., p. 296.

31. *Khrushchev Remembers*, p. 222.

32. *Memoirs*, pp. 297-98.

33. A. Chandler and S. E. Ambrose, eds., *Eisenhower Papers: The War Years*, p. 2683.

34. New York, 1961.

35. B. Gardner, *Year that Changed the World*, p. 144.

36. *Memoirs*, p. 300.

37. *Eisenhower Papers: The War Years*, p. 2683.

38. Letter to the author, November 27, 1971.

39. Pages 206-207.

40. Doenitz interview in *Die Welt*, April 29, 1975.

41. Loc. cit.

42. W. Strang, *Britain in World Affairs*, p. 339.

43. W. Laqueur, *Russia and Germany: A Century of Conflict*, p. 273.

44. *House of Commons Debates*, 5th Series, Vol. 535 (1954-55), pp. 15879-1580.

45. R. Ingersoll, *Top Secret*, p. 321.

46. New York *Times*, November 24, 1954.

BIBLIOGRAPHY

Primary (Published and Unpublished Documents, Microfilm, Papers and Letters)

Beitzell, R., ed., *Tehran, Yalta, Potsdam, the Soviet Protocols.* Hattiesburg, Miss.: Academic International, 1970.

Doenitz Collection, N236. Militaergeschichtliches Forschungsamt, Freiburg im Breisgau, Federal Republic of Germany.

Foreign Relations of the United States. *1943,* Vol. III. Washington, D.C.: U.S. Government Printing Office, 1963.

———. *The Conferences at Washington and Quebec, 1943.* Washington, D.C.: U.S. Government Printing Office, 1970.

———. *The Conferences at Cairo and Tehran, 1943.* Washington, D.C.: U.S. Government Printing Office, 1961.

———. *The Conference at Quebec, 1944.* Washington, D.C.: U.S. Government Printing Office, 1972.

———. *The Conferences at Malta and Yalta, 1945.* Washington, D.S.: U.S. Government Printing Office, 1955.

———. *The Conference of Berlin (The Potsdam Conference), 1945.* Washington, D.C.: U.S. Governmt Printing Office, 1960.

———. *Diplomatic Papers, 1945,* Vol. III, *European Advisory Commission; Austria; Germany.* Washington, D.C.: U.S. Government Printing Office, 1968.

———. *Council of Foreign Ministers, 1946,* Vol. II. Washington, D.C.: U.S. Government Printing Office, 1970.

German Records Microfilmed at Alexandria, Va. Guide 18, Reels 858, 859, 860, 864 and 867.

Great Britain. Public Records Office. Foreign Office documents 371/46775/C9272, C8792, C9001, C8987, C9003, C9141, C9177, C9244, and 371/46776/C9509, C9603, C9657, C9668, C9855, C9668, C9857, C9979.

———. War Cabinet Minutes. War Cabinet 58(45), 4 May 1945.

———. War Office. "Papers of Field Marshal Alexander," 214/42, File No. 17, Vol. III.

House of Commons Debates. 5th Series, Vol. 535 (1954-55).

Kuby, E., *Das Ende des Schreckens: Dokumente des Untergangs, Januar bis Mai 1945.* Muenchen: Sueddeutscher Verlag, 1955.

Letter to author. Dr. Brausch, June 18, 1973.

———. Karl Doenitz, November 27, 1971.

———. S. L. A. Marshall, August 30, 1971.

———. Norwegian Armed Forces, the Historical Department, April 4, 1972.

Maschke, E., ed. *Zur Geschichte der deutschen Kriegsgefangen des Zweiten Weltkrieges.* 22 vols. Muenchen: Verlag Ernst und Werner Gieseking, 1967.

Nazi Conspiracy and Aggression. Supplement B. Washington, D.C.: U.S. Government Printing Office, 1946.

Oppen, B. R., von, ed., *Documents on Germany under Occupation, 1945-1954.* New York: Oxford University Press, 1955.

Quellen der Institut fuer Zeitgeschichte, Munich, unpublished manuscripts. Archive No. 160, Kurt von Tippelskirsch, Akz. Nr. 785/52, 00037; Archive No. 1740, Eberhard Godt, 3190/63; and Archive No. 1765, Joachim Schultz, 2479/59.

United States, Department of State. *Occupation of Germany, Policy and Progress, 1945-46.* Washington, D.C.: U.S. Government Printing Office, 1947.

United States, National Archives. "Foreign military studies, 1945-1954," with Supplement. Series number MS# P-202; MS# B-328; MS# B-361; MS# B-125; MS# B-554; and MS# C-049.

United States, Records of the U.S. Joint Chiefs of Staff. CCS 334 Combined Chiefs of Staff (8-17-43), 113th Meeting ("9. Military Considerations in Relation to Russia"), RG 218.

Primary (Books and Articles)

Adenauer, K., *Memoirs, 1945-1953.* Chicago: Henry Regnery, 1966.

Alexander, H., *The Alexander Memoirs, 1940-1945.* London: McGraw-Hill, 1962.

Asquith, Baroness. "Baroness Asquith of Yarnbury in conversation with Kenneth Harris," *The Listener,* August 17, 1967, pp. 197-200.

Beneš, E., *Memoirs of Dr. Eduard Beneš.* Boston: Houghton Mifflin, 1953.

Bialer, S., ed., *Stalin and His Generals: Soviet Military Memoirs of World War II.* New York: Pegasus, 1969.

Blumenson, M., *The Patton Papers, 1940-1945.* Boston: Houghton Mifflin, 1974.

Boldt, G., *Die Letzen Tage der Reichskanzlei.* Stuttgart: Rowohlt Verlag, 1947.

Bradley, O., *A Soldier's Story.* New York: Henry Holt, 1951.

Bryant, A., *The Turn of the Tide, 1939-1943.* London: Collins, 1957.

———, *Triumph in the West.* New York: Doubleday, 1959.

Bullitt, W., "How we won the war and lost the peace," *Life Magazine,* August 30, 1948, p. 94.

Butcher, H. C., *My Three Years with Eisenhower.* New York: Simon and Schuster, 1946.

Byrnes, J. F., *All in One Lifetime.* New York: Harper and Brothers, 1947.

———, *Speaking Frankly.* New York: Harper and Brothers, 1947.

Chandler, A. D. and S. E. Ambrose, eds., *The Papers of Dwight D. Eisenhower: The War Years.* Baltimore: Johns Hopkins, 1969.

Churchill, R. S., ed., *The Sinews of Peace: Post-War Speeches by Winston Churchill.* Boston: Houghton Mifflin, 1949.

———, *The Unwritten Alliance: Speeches 1953 to 1959 by Winston S. Churchill.* London: Cassell, 1961.

Churchill, W. S., *The Hinge of Fate.* Boston: Houghton Mifflin, 1950.

———, *Triumph and Tragedy.* Boston: Houghton Mifflin, 1950.

Ciechanowski, J., *Defeat in Victory.* New York: Doubleday, 1942.

Clark, M., *Calculated Risk.* New York: Harper and Brothers, 1950.

Clay, L. D., *Decision in Germany.* New York: Doubleday, 1950.

Cooper, D., *Old Men Forget.* London: Rupert Hart-Davis, 1954.

Dalton, H., *The Fateful Years: Memoirs 1931-1945.* London: Frederick Muller, 1957.

Dilks, D., ed., *The Diaries of Sir Alexander Cadogan, 1938-1945.* New York: G. P. Putnam, 1972.

Eden, A., *The Memoirs of Anthony Eden: The Reckoning.* Boston: Houghton Mifflin, 1965.

Eisenhower, D. D., *Crusade in Europe.* New York: Doubleday, 1961.

Flower, D. and J. Reeves, eds., *The Taste of Courage: Victory and Defeat.* New York: Berkley Medallion Ed., 1971.

Granzow, K., *Tagebuch eines Hitlerjungen, 1943-1945.* Bremen: C. Schuenemann, 1965.

Guingand, F. de, *Operation Victory.* London: Hodder and Stoughton, 1948.

Harriman, A. and E. Abel, *Special Envoy to Churchill and Stalin, 1941-1946.* New York: Random House, 1975.

Ismay, H., *The Memoirs of General Lord Ismay.* New York: Viking, 1960.

Kaestner, E., *Notebene 45, Ein Tagebuch.* Zurich: Atrium Verlag, 1961.

Keitel, W., *Memoirs.* New York: Stein and Day, 1966.

Kennedy, J., *The Business of War.* London: Hutchinson, 1957.

Kersten, F., *The Kersten Memoirs, 1940-1945.* New York: Macmillan, 1957.

Khrushchev, N., *Khrushchev Remembers.* Boston: Little, Brown, 1970.

Kirkpatrick, I., *The Inner Circle.* London: Macmillan, 1959.

Kleist, P., *The European Tragedy.* Isle of Man: Times Press, 1965.

Koller, K., *Der Letze Monat.* Mannheim: Norbert Wohlgemuth Verlag, 1949.

Kopp, F., *Chronik der Wiederbewaffnung in Deutschland.* Koeln: Markus Verlag, 1958.

Leahy, W. D., *I was There.* New York: McGraw-Hill, 1950.

Leasor, J., *War at the Top.* London: Michael Joseph, 1959.

Loewenheim, F. L., H. D. Langley and M. Jones, eds., *Roosevelt and Churchill: Their Secret Wartime Correspondence.* New York: Saturday Review Press, 1975.

Luedde-Neurath, W., *Regierung Doenitz.* Goettingen: Musterschmidt, 1950.

MacMillan, H., *The Blast of War, 1939-1945.* New York: Macmillan, 1966.

Millis, W., ed., *The Forrestal Diaries.* New York: Viking Press, 1951.

Molotov, V. M., *Problems of Foreign Policy: Speeches and Statements, April 1945-November 1948.* Moscow: Foreign Language Publishing House, 1949.

Montgomery, B. L., *The Memoirs of Field Marshal, The Viscount Montgomery.* New York: World Publishing Co., 1958.

– – –, *Normandy to the Baltic.* London: Hutchinson, n.d.

– – –, "Russia's rising military might," *U.S. News and World Report,* Vol. 26, No. 23 (June 4, 1954), p. 45.

Moran, C., *Churchill: Taken from the Diaries of Lord Moran.* Boston: Houghton Mifflin, 1966.

Morgan, F., *Overture to Overlord.* New York: Doubleday, 1950.

Morgenthau Diary. Vol. II. Washington, D.C.: U.S. Government Printing Office, 1967.

Murphy, R., *Diplomat Among Warriors.* New York: Pyramid, 1965.

Nelson, J., ed., *A Conversation with Alistair Cooke: General Eisenhower on the Military Churchill.* New York: W. W. Norton, 1970.

Patton, G. S., *War As I Knew It.* Boston: Houghton Mifflin, 1947.

Rahn, R., *Ruheloses Leben.* Duesseldorf: Diederichs Verlag, 1949.

Ridgeway, M. B., *Soldier: The Memoirs of Matthew B. Ridgeway.* New York: Harper and Brothers, 1956.

Roosevelt, E., *As He Saw It.* New York: Duell, Sloan and Pearce, 1946.

Schultz, J., *Die Letzten 30 Tage.* Stuttgart: Steingrueben Verlag, 1951.

Sherwood, R. E., *Roosevelt and Hopkins: An Intimate History.* New York: Harper and Brothers, 1948.

Smith, J. E., ed., *The Papers of General Lucius D. Clay*. Bloomington: Indiana University Press, 1974.
Stimson, H. L. and M. Bundy. *On Active Service*. New York: Harper and Brothers, 1948.
Strang, W., *Home and Abroad*. London: André Deutsch, 1956.
Tàborský, E., "Beneš and Stalin—Moscow, 1943 and 1945," *Journal of Central European Affairs*, XIII (July 1953), pp. 145-181.
Templewood, Viscount, *Complacent Dictator*. New York: Alfred A. Knopf, 1947.
Truman, H. S., *Memoirs*. Vol. I. New York: Signet, 1965.
Vandenberg, A. H., Jr., ed., *Private Papers of Senator Vandenberg*. Boston: Houghton Mifflin, 1952.
Vansittart, Lord R. G., *Bones of Contention*. New York: Alfred A. Knopf, 1945.
Vital Speeches of the Day, XII (March 15, 1946), p. 331.
Warlimont, W., *Inside Hitler's Headquarters, 1939-1945*. New York: Frederick A. Praeger, 1964.
Wedemeyer, A. C., *Wedemeyer Reports*. New York: Henry Holt, 1958.
Williams, F., *A Prime Minister Remembers*. London: Heinemann, 1961.
Zhukov, G., *The Memoirs of Marshal Zhukov*. London: Delacorte, 1971.

Secondary (Books and Articles)

Adams, H. H., *1942: The Year that Doomed the Axis*. New York: David McKay, 1967.
Alperovitz, G., *Atomic Diplomacy: Hiroshima and Potsdam*. London: Secker and Warburg, 1966.
— — —, "How did the Cold War begin?" *New York Review of Books*, VII (March 23, 1967), 6-12.
Anderson, E., "Germany in the Cold War," *Survey* 58 (January 1966), 1961.
Armstrong, A., *Unconditional Surrender*. New Jersey: Rutgers University Press, 1961.
Baldwin, H., *Great Mistakes of the War*. New York: Harper and Brothers, 1950.
Balfour, M., "Another look at 'Unconditional Surrender,' " *International Affairs*, Vol. 46, No. 4 (October 1970), 719-737.
— — — and J. Mair, *Four-Power Control in Germany and Austria, 1945-1946*. New York: Oxford University Press, 1956.
Barnett, C., *Britain and Her Army, 1509-1970*. New York: Morrow, 1970.
Bartlett, C. J. *The Long Retreat: A Short History of British Defense Policy, 1945-1970*. London: Macmillan, 1972.
Bauer, K., *Deutsche Verteidigungspolitik, 1948-1967*. Boppard am Rhein: Harald Boldt Verlag, 1968.
Beitzell, R., *The Uneasy Alliance*. New York: Alfred A. Knopf, 1972.
Bekker, C., *Kampf und Untergang der Kriegsmarine*. Hannover: Adolf Sponholtz Verlag, 1953.
Bernstein, B. J., ed., *Politics and Policies of the Truman Administration*. Chicago: Quadrangle, 1970.
Bezymenski, L., *The Death of Adolf Hitler: Unknown Documents from Soviet Archives*. New York: Harcourt, Brace and World, 1968.
Burchett, W. G., *Cold War in Germany*. Melbourne, Australia: World Unity Publications, 1950.
Burns, J., *Roosevelt: The Soldier of Freedom*. New York: Harcourt Brace Jovanovich, 1970.
Campbell, J. C., *The United States in World Affairs, 1945-1947*. New York: Harper and Brothers, 1947.

Chase, J. L., "Unconditional surrender reconsidered," *Political Science Quarterly,* LXX, No. 2 (June 1955), 258-279.

Clemens, D. S., *Yalta.* New York: Oxford University Press, 1970.

Coles, H. and A. K. Weinberg, *Civil Affairs: Soldiers Become Governors.* Washington, D.C.: U.S. Government Printing Office, 1964.

Cookridge, E. H., *Gehlen: Spy of the Century.* London: Transworld Publishers, 1972.

Cornides, W., *Die Weltmaechte und Deutschland: Geschichte der juengsten Vergangenheit, 1945-1955.* Tuebingen: R Wunderlich, 1961.

Craig, G., *NATO and the New German Army.* Princeton: Princeton Center of International Studies, 1955.

Crawley, A., *The Spoils of War: The Rise of Western Germany Since 1945.* New York: Bobbs-Merrill, 1973.

Crozier, B., *Franco.* Boston: Little, Brown, 1967.

Dallin, A., "Vlasov and separate peace: a note," *Journal of Central European Affairs,* XVI (January 1957), 394-396.

Daniels, W., *Defense of Western Europe.* New York: H. W. Wilson, 1950.

Daugherty, W. and M. Janowitz, *A Psychological Warfare Casebook.* Baltimore: John Hopkins, 1968.

Davidson, E., *The Death and Life of Germany.* New York: Alfred A. Knopf, 1959.

Deakin, F. W., *The Brutal Friendship.* New York: Anchor, 1966.

Deutscher, I., *Ironies of History: Essays on Contemporary Communism.* London: Oxford University Press, 1966.

Divine, R., ed., *Causes and Consequences of World War II.* Chicago: Quadrangle, 1969.

Druks, H., *Harry S Truman and the Russians, 1945-1953.* New York: Robert Speller, 1966.

Dulles, A., *The Secret Surrender.* New York: Harper and Row, 1966.

Dulles, J. F., *Our Policy for Germany.* Washington, D.C.: U.S. Government Printing Office, 1954.

Erdmann, J. M., *Leaflet Operations in the Second World War.* Denver: Denver Instant Printing, 1969.

Essame, H., *The Battle for Germany.* New York: Scribner's, 1969.

Feis, H., *From Trust to Terror: The Onset of the Cold War, 1945-1950.* New York: W. W. Norton, 1970.

———, *Churchill, Roosevelt, and Stalin.* Princeton: Princeton University Press, 1957.

Fitzsimmons, M., *Foreign Policy of the British Labor Government, 1945-1951.* Notre Dame, Indiana: University of Notre Dame Press, 1953.

Gaddis, J. L., *The United States and the Origins of the Cold War, 1941-1948.* New York: Columbia University Press, 1972.

Gallagher, M. P., *The Soviet History of World War II.* London: Praeger, 1963.

Gardner, B., *Churchill in Power: As Seen by His Contemporaries.* Boston: Houghton Mifflin, 1970.

———, *The Year That Changed the World, 1945.* New York: Coward-McCann, 1964.

Hagen, L., *The Secret War for Europe.* New York: Stein and Day, 1969.

Hankey, Lord, "Unconditional surrender," *The Contemporary Review,* Vol. 176 (October 1949), 197-198.

Higgins, T., *Winston Churchill and the Second Front, 1940-1943.* London. Oxford University Press, 1957.

Hill, R., *Struggle for Germany.* New York: Harper and Brothers, 1947.

Howe, Q., *Ashes of Victory.* New York: Simon and Schuster, 1972.

Ingersoll, R., *Top Secret.* New York: Harcourt Brace and Co., 1946.

Ingram, K., *History of the Cold War.* London: Darwen Finlayson, 1955.

Jansen, T., *Abruestung und Deutschland-Frage: Die Abruestungsfrage als Problem der deutschen Aussenpolitik.* Mainz: Hase u. Koehler Verlag, 1968.

Jones, J. M., *The Fifteen Weeks.* New York: Viking, 1955.

Kecskemeti, P., *Strategic Surrender.* Stanford: Stanford University Press, 1958.

Keesing's Contemporary Archives. London: Keesing's Publications, 1946.

Keesing's Research Report. *Germany and Eastern Europe Since 1945.* New York: Scribner's, 1973.

Kempner, R. M. K., "Stalin's 'Separate Peace' in 1943," *United Nations World,* 4 (March 1950). 7-9.

Kirchner, K., ed., *Flugblaetter aus England.* Erlangen: Verlag fuer Zeitgeschichte, 1974.

–––, *Flugblattpropaganda in 2. Weltkrieg.* Muenchen: Verlag fuer Zeitgeschichte, 1972.

Koch, H. W., "The spectre of a separate peace in the east: Russo-German 'peace feelers,' 1942-1944," *Journal of Contemporary History,* 19:3 (July 1975), 531-549.

Kochan, L., *The Struggle for Germany, 1918-1945.* Edinburgh: Edinburgh University Press, 1963.

Kolko, G., *The Politics of War.* New York: Random House, 1968.

Krantkraemer, E., *Deutsche Geschichte nach dem zweiten Weltkrieg.* Hildesheim: August Lax, 1972.

Kuby, E., *The Russians and Berlin: 1945.* New York: Ballantine, 1969.

Laqueur, W., *Russia and Germany: A Century of Conflict.* Boston: Little, Brown, 1965.

Lewis, G. and J. Mewha. *History of Prisoner of War Utilization by the United States Army, 1776-1945.* Washington, D.C.: U.S. Government Printing Office, 1955.

Lerner, D., *Sykewar: Psychological Warfare Against Germany, D-Day to VE-Day.* New York: George W. Stewart, 1949.

Linebarger, P. M., *Psychological Warfare.* Washington, D.C.: Combat Forces Press, 1954.

Liddell-Hart, B. H., *History of the Second World War.* New York: G. P. Putnam, 1971.

Luard, E., ed., *The Cold War: A Re-appraisal.* New York: Frederick A. Praeger, 1964.

Manstein, E. von. *Verlorene Seige.* Bonn: Athenaeum, 1955.

Mastny, V., "Stalin and the prospects of a separate peace in World War II," *The American Historical Review,* Vol. 77, No. 5 (December 1972), 1365-1388.

Matloff, M., "The Soviet Union and the war in the west," in *American History: Recent Interpretations,* Bk. II, ed. by A. Eisenstadt. New York: Thomas Y. Crowell, 1962.

Mayne, R., *The Recovery of Europe, 1945-1973.* New York: Anchor, 1973.

McGeehan, R., *German Rearmament Question: American Diplomacy and Europe after World War II.* Glencoe, Ill.: University of Illinois Press, 1971.

McNeill, W. H., *America, Britain and Russia.* New York: Oxford University Press, 1953.

Mee, Jr., C. L., *Meeting at Potsdam.* New York: M. Evans, 1975.

Meehan, E., *The British Left Wing and Foreign Policy.* New Brunswick, N.J.: Rutgers University Press, 1960.

Meissner, B., *Russland, die Westmaechte und Deutschland.* Hamburg: H. H. Noelke Verlag, 1953.

Middleton, D., *The Defense of Western Europe.* New York: Appleton-Century-Crofts, 1952.

–––, "Germany played for time at Reims," New York *Times,* May 9, 1945.

Mikolajczyk, S., *The Pattern of Soviet Domination.* London: Marston, 1948.

Miksche, F. O., *Unconditional Surrender: The Roots of World War III.* London: Faber and Faber, 1952.

Morison, S. E., *Strategy and Compromise.* Boston: Little, Brown, 1958.

Moorehead, A., *Eclipse.* New York: Harper and Row, 1968.

Morgan, R., *The United States and West Germany, 1945-1973.* London: Oxford University Press, 1974.

Morray, J. P., *From Yalta to Disarmament: Cold War Debate.* New York: MR Press, 1961.

Mueller, J., *Sturz in der Abgrund: Die Letzte 10 Monate von 20 Juli '44 bis zum 8 Mai '45.* Offenbach am Main: Bollwerk Verlag, 1947.

Nano, F. C., "The first Soviet double cross," *Journal of Central European Affairs,* Vol. 12, No. 3 (October 1952), 236-258.

Nettl, J. P., *The Eastern Zone and Soviet Policy in Germany, 1945 50.* London: Oxford University Press, 1951.

Neumann, W. L., *After Victory: Churchill, Roosevelt, Stalin and the Making of the Peace.* New York: Harper and Row, 1967.

North, J., *Northwest Europe, 1944-1945.* London: Her Majesty's Stationary Office, 1953.

Penrose, E. F., "Negotiating on refugees and displaced persons, 1946," in *Negotiating with the Russians,* R. Dennett and J. E. Johnson, eds. Boston: World Peace Foundation, 1951.

Pogue, F. C., *George C. Marshall: Organizer of Victory, 1943-1945.* New York: Viking, 1973.

———, *Supreme Command.* Washington, D.C.: U.S. Government Printing Office, 1954.

Pritt, D. N., *The Labour Government, 1945-51.* New York: International Publishers, 1963.

Rauch, G. von, *A History of Soviet Russia.* New York: Frederick A. Praeger, 1957.

Ritter, G., *The German Resistance.* New York: Frederick A. Praeger, 1958.

Root, W., *Casablanca to Katyn: The Secret History of the War.* New York: Scribner's, 1946.

Rose, L. A., *After Yalta.* New York: Scribner's, 1973.

Rozek, E. J., *Allied Wartime Diplomacy: A Pattern in Poland.* New York: John Wiley, 1958.

Ryan, C., *The Last Battle.* New York: Simon and Schuster, 1966.

Schlamm, W. S., *Germany and the East-West Crisis.* New York: David McKay, 1959.

Schoenfeld, M. P., *The War Ministry of Winston Churchill.* Ames, Iowa: Iowa State University Press, 1972.

Schubert, K. von, *Wiederbewaffnung und Westintegration.* Stuttgart: Deutsche Verlags-Anstalt, 1970.

Seabury, P., "Cold War origins I," *The Journal of Contemporary History,* Vol. 3, No. 1 (January 1968), 169-182.

———, *The Rise and Decline of the Cold War.* New York: Basic Books, 1967.

Sereny, G., *Into That Darkness.* New York: McGraw-Hill, 1947.

Sharp, T., *The Wartime Alliance and the Zonal Division of Germany.* Oxford: Clarendon, 1975.

Sherwin, M. J., *A World Destroyed: The Atomic Bomb and the Grand Alliance.* New York: Alfred A. Knopf, 1973.

Shils, E. A. and M. Janowitz, "Cohesion and disintegration in the Wehrmacht in World War II," *Public Opinion Quarterly,* Summer 1948, 280-315.

Slawin, L. J., *Die Letzten Tage des "Dritten Reiches."* Berlin: Verlag "Lied der Zeit," 1948.

Smith, A. L., Jr., "Churchill et l'armée allemande, 1945," *Revue d'histoire de la deuxième guerre mondial,* 93 (January 1974), 65-78.

———, "Life in wartime Germany," *The Public Opinion Quarterly,* Vol. 36 (Spring 1972), 1-7.

Smith, W. B., *Eisenhower's Six Great Decisions: Europe 1944-1945.* New York: Longmans, 1956.

Stein, H., ed., *American Civil-Military Decisions.* Birmingham, Ala.: University of Alabama Press, 1963.

Steinert, M. G., *Hitlers Krieg und die Deutschen.* Duesseldorf: Econ Verlag, 1970.

———, *23 Days: The Final Collapse of Nazi Germany.* New York: Walker, 1969.

Strang, W., *Britain in World Affairs.* New York: Frederick A. Praeger, 1961.

Taylor, A. J. P., *English History, 1914-1945.* New York: Oxford University Press, 1965.

Theoharis, A., "Roosevelt and Truman on Yalta: the origins of the Cold War," *Political Science Quarterly,* Vol. LXXXVII, No. 2 (June 1972), 210-241.

Thompson, C., *The Assassination of Winston Churchill.* Buckinghamshire: Colin Smythe, 1969.

Thompson, R. W., *Churchill and the Montgomery Myth.* New York: M. Evans, 1967.

———, *Montgomery, The Field Marshal: The Campaign in North-West Europe, 1944-1945.* New York: Scribner's, 1969.

Thorwald, J., *Das Ende an der Elbe.* Stuttgart: Steingrueben-Verlag, 1953.

———, *Es Begann an der Weichsel.* Stuttgart: Steingrueben-Verlag, 1953.

———, *The Illusion: Soviet Soldiers in Hitler's Armies.* New York: Viking, 1972.

Ulam, A. B., *The Rivals, America and Russia Since World War II.* New York: Viking, 1972.

Umiastowski, R., *Poland, Russia and Great Britain, 1941-1945.* London: Hollis and Carter, 1945.

Volle, H. and C.-J. Duisberg, *Probleme der Internationalen Abruestung.* Frankfurt A.M.: Alfred Metzner Verlag, 1964.

Waldman, E., *The Goose Step is Verboten: The German Army Today.* New York: Free Press, 1964.

Warner, A. L., "Our secret deal over Germany," *Saturday Evening Post,* August 2, 1952, p. 30.

———, *Germany—Bridge or Battleground?* London: Heinemann, 1947.

Watt, D. C., *Britain Looks to Germany: British Opinion and Policy Towards Germany Since 1945.* London: Oswald Wolff, 1965.

Werth, A., *The Year of Stalingrad.* New York: Alfred A. Knopf, 1947.

Wheeler-Bennett, J. and A. Nichols, *The Semblance of Peace.* New York: St. Martin's, 1972.

Whiting, C., *The End of the War, Europe: April 15-May 23, 1945.* New York: Stein and Day, 1973.

Willenz, E., "Early discussions regarding a defense contribution in Germany, 1948-1950," U.S. Air Force Project, Rand Research Memo. 968, *German Studies.* Santa Monica, Calif.: Rand, 1952.

Wolfe, T. W., *Soviet Power and Europe, 1945-1970.* Baltimore: John Hopkins, 1970.

Woodward, L., *British Foreign Policy in the Second World War.* Vol. III. London: H.M.S.O., 1971.

Ziemke, E. F., *The German Northern Theater of Operations, 1940-1945.* Washington, D.C.: Dept. of Army Pamphlet 20-271, n.d.

Newspapers

Deutsche Allgemeine Zeitung   *Neue Rhein Zeitung*
Christ and Welt   New York *Times*
Economist   *Rhein Neckar Zeitung*
Heidelberger Tageblatt   *Times* (London)
Los Angeles *Times*   *Voelkischer Beobachter*
Manchester *Guardian*   *Die Welt*

INDEX

ABOUT THE AUTHOR

ARTHUR L. SMITH, Jr. is Professor of History at California State University, Los Angeles and Curator of the Center for the Study of Armament and Disarmament at the same institution. After studies in America and Switzerland, he served the U.S. government as an Assistant to the Adjutant General's Office, Bremerhaven, Germany, 1947-1949. In 1956 he received his Ph.D. from the University of Southern California. Dr. Smith has published extensively on primarily disarmament and twentieth-century German history. Among his monographs and articles are *The Deutschtum of Nazi Germany and the United States* (The Hague: Martinus Nijhoff, 1965); "Le désarmement de l'Allemagne en 1919," *Revue Historique*, CCXXVIII (July 1962); and "History Writing and World War II," *General Military Review*, 9 (November 1969).